HEAVEN'S OPEN DOOR

SANDRA ORLANDO

BALBOA.
PRESS

A DIVISION OF HAY HOUSE

Balboa Press books may be ordered through booksellers or by contacting:

Balboa Press
A Division of Hay House
1663 Liberty Drive
Bloomington, IN 47403
www.balboapress.com
1 (877) 407-4847

Because of the dynamic nature of the Internet, any web addresses or links contained in this book may have changed since publication and may no longer be valid. The views expressed in this work are solely those of the author and do not necessarily reflect the views of the publisher, and the publisher hereby disclaims any responsibility for them.

The author of this book does not dispense medical advice or prescribe the use of any technique as a form of treatment for physical, emotional, or medical problems without the advice of a physician, either directly or indirectly. The intent of the author is only to offer information of a general nature to help you in your quest for emotional and spiritual well-being. In the event you use any of the information in this book for yourself, which is your constitutional right, the author and the publisher assume no responsibility for your actions.

Any people depicted in stock imagery provided by Thinkstock are models, and such images are being used for illustrative purposes only. Certain stock imagery © Thinkstock.

Printed in the United States of America.

ISBN: 978-1-4525-9934-2 (sc)
ISBN: 978-1-4525-9935-9 (e)

Balboa Press rev. date: 12/05/2014

HEAVEN'S OPEN DOOR....
as experienced by...

The Gospel According to Sandra

Everything I have learned has only brought me
to the realization of just how much I don't know
and how wide open is the door to more.

Why I Am Writing This Book..... It was not an easy decision
to write for God. I argued and argued with myself about my
own credibility. I questioned my abilities as far as being a
writer even, compared to those who were great and inspiring
authors. After taking my insecurities to prayer I heard God to
say, *"Did I not say to go forth and preach the good news?"* God
told me **everyone** has a gospel inside to share. I realized that
the language and the telling of my experiences are within the
confines of who and what I am as a personality both formed
and reformed again and again and it was alright. My approach
to life had always seemed prior to this book, as a dove, a
peacemaker, a caring person, a diplomatic and non-aggressive
personality. I understand however, there are many approaches,
but God honors each person's intentions and each person's
heart over one's perceived abilities. In prayer I began to use the
"Our Father" prayer described in the gospels especially when I
was questioning just what was the "Will of God" and pondered
what "God" maybe wanted to have happen as opposed to my
limited vision. I learned how to pray for a person's "highest
good" as an alternative in prayer. The "Our Father" Jesus said
was the perfect prayer so how was I to improve on that?

Who Am I? I am a 73 year old witness to the God in my life. I lived in Cincinnati, Ohio for all of my life. I was the oldest of 4 children, raised Roman Catholic, attended Catholic schools, went to college two years for an Associate Degree in Business, got a job, fell in love, married and had children. I am happy and love being here on Earth and also part of a very large family.

I have 13 children (yes, same father) and am a grandmother and then great grandmother to around 70 in number. It wasn't an easy road all the time but I loved it even the struggles (mostly after they were over and saw the whole picture). After 28 years of marriage I divorced. We are both still friends today and I love the gift that we can still see the goodness in each other. Today I am still busy living life as it shows up with some new challenge every day. The good news is today that I live it with the help of God and the angels. Through the years I have found out who I am and who I am not (I do not know which one comes first, they are interchangeable) The reference point, on who I am has ripened through the years I might add.

I retired from Children's Hospital after 20 years. I worked as an Administrative Secretary in both Infectious Diseases and Holistic Health. In between time growing up as I call it, besides being a mom of many, I volunteered as a grief counselor, youth worker, Right-To-Life advocate, and additionally volunteered through my church and community in different capacities. Later in life I pursued community within the Native American way of life as an addition to my

Christian background, embracing my spirituality. To this day I still hold near my heart, many Native American values and insights

The Beginning of Our Story: I have always enjoyed writing and this being my first published serious attempt I hope to tell our story (God's, the angels and mine) in the anticipation that it may make a delightful difference in some way to give glory to the Great I Am (God as I call Him). It's about my spiritual journey and the progression of events that have led me to the awakening I realize today.

Note: Throughout the book God's words or those of the angels are usually italicized to bring emphasis.

My spiritual awareness in life started in my late 20's with a Catholic 4-day women's retreat. It changed my life. I walked away knowing that something extraordinary had happened. I had met up with the Spirit of God and this changed to a great extent my life's focus. It wasn't a head trip it was a heart trip. After that weekend I could not stop reading the scriptures or praying and my life took on new meanings and new understandings. It was the realization of the love of God and the reality of a divine relationship that added immensely to the magnitude of my life. This different reality laid before me a path of discoveries of a world beyond what we could only see, taste and feel. It led me to a reality of certainties beyond anything I could put together myself. I was later directed to share these writings and to start putting them down on paper. These writings usually took place in the early morning hours, getting me up out of bed and to the journals and computer.

I am yet no expert on the angels that appeared. I had no wild plans for my life. I just lived life every day as it showed up on my doorstep. But....Something wonderful happened one day just out of the blue and I wish to share it with you.

That something in the first part of this book is related to personal witness. The second part is related to lessons given by the Great I Am and different angels as named. **The message of this book is extraordinary events can happen to very ordinary people because we are all extraordinary.** Everything in the gospels tell us this all the time. I wish only to give testimony that normal does not really exist. I still am no saint but it is OK and I feel it is OK because God first named us "Beloved" as He told me and loves me right where I am. So, here goes the stories and witnesses that validate a divine relationship we all engage in whether we know it or not. This is, as of sorts, a documentary over the last 30 years.

Before I begin my journey with the angels, let me insert a post script here. When I make a gender identification related to a particular angel like "Him" or "Her" I am referring to the energy that I myself, identify as masculine or feminine. This is related to my environmental upbringing. Angels are genderless and the Creator is everything, so no harm or prejudice intended. It is just my way of describing the energy. Sometimes I refer to God as God and sometimes Creator and sometimes The Source or The Great I Am. These three names are my familiars. No elimination is intended.

My First Encounter - The Archangel Raphael

It was in the Spring of 1981. Peg, a friend, and I both lived in a neighborhood called Winton Place, Ohio. Many New Jerusalem Community members, like Peg's family and mine often came together for community, prayer and teachings under the pastoral care of Father Richard Rohr, a Franciscan priest. The New Jerusalem Community, a Catholic lay community, was a central part of my life for many years. This is Peg's and my story, our story: It was an ordinary day, kids off to school, cleaned house, fixed dinner, cleaned up dishes and off to visit with Peg who lived down the hill.

The witness begins when Peg Benton, now McGee, asked me to come over to pray with her because she wanted to stop smoking. It was a natural request because Peg and I often functioned as prayer partners for each other within the community for various reasons. We decided to go to her house to pray because the kids were running all over at my house. I had 13 children and Peg has 2 so the odds of getting in some prayer time uninterrupted were better at her home.

We prayed together in the ordinary way, hands folded and looking up asking God to help us. After prayers I decided to stay and visit for awhile like friends do. I was leisurely standing in her hallway looking at her hermit crabs in her aquarium when sudden chill came over me.

It was a summer evening and it was hot. Peg's fan was blowing down the hallway but not directly on me. I felt a bone chilling cold that seemed to come from inside me not from a fan blowing outside on me. It happened several times over the next hour and each time I grew colder and colder. I thought perhaps that I was getting sick so Peg suggested that I lay down on the couch and offered to make me a hot cup of tea. While she was in the kitchen as I was lying there on her couch with a light blanket, suddenly without warning a misty figure of a young man stood at my side next to the couch. He was dressed in a very soft, hazy white tunic. The glow around him seemed soft but I could see every color in its glow. My eyes were first attracted to this haze that encircled his whole body Then I looked at his face. He was just standing there smiling and then he spoke. I was not afraid for some reason because his voice was so soft almost like music. With this smile on his face he said, "Do not be afraid, my name is Raphael and I have been sent as a messenger from God and I have come to heal and bind spirits. Go tell your priest that I am here." Then as quickly as he appeared he disappeared.

It took me a moment to what I call wake up (although my eyes were not closed) and regain my composure. It must have been a dream I thought to myself but I had no recollection of falling asleep or waking up. Peg reentered the room with a cup of hot steaming tea and she must have noticed the look on my face. She asked if I was alright. I remember saying, "I don't think so." As Peg sat down in the chair across from me I started telling her what had just happened. My description of the figure was, " it was as if an angel or ghost was standing in front of me". I commented that I wasn't sure exactly what had happened and I could think of no other analogy to use. After I had finished she began to share with me a similar experience that had recently happened to her at work that week.

She worked for her brother who owned and operated a wholesale meat packaging warehouse. Peg stocked the freezers and filled the orders as well as did some of the office work. She entered the freezer to stock as usual one day and out of the corner of her eye she caught a glimpse of a huge figure standing in the corner of the freezer. She had just enough of a glance to notice that the very tall figure was surrounded by a bluish light A more curious part of the puzzle was that she recalled that he had three sets of wings so later supposed him to be an angel but like me dismissed it as stress or some moment of insanity. The two sets of larger wings were joined at his back with one smaller set that crossed in front. She remarked that he did not say anything but just disappeared. She remarked half joking that no wonder he was blue he was standing in a freezer. Unknown to me at the time she had shared this information with another community member later who had cautioned her to keep this information to herself.

We both speculated whether the two incidences were somehow related. I had never before seen an angel or what could be construed as an angel or had this kind of experience. (I think

Peg had some experiences when she was a child). The wings on the figure told her that it must be an angel. My figure had no wings just this glow about him but I had a name, Raphael. Out of curiosity we decided to try to find a book on angels at the New Jerusalem library down the street that day but with no such luck. Still sort of reeling from the experience I later went home to fix dinner. I was quiet that night and kept the details to myself still pondering whether the two incidences were connected somehow or whether they were even real. A few days passed and I kept myself pretty busy

The next angelic confirmation came the next Saturday. Peg breathlessly came to my side door and she was definitely excited about something. When I opened the door she shoved this xeroxed paper in my hands and told me to look at it. I looked at the picture. I could feel the tears welling up in my eyes. It was a portrayal of the "6-winged angel named Raphael." I did not even read the text because I was filled with awe and began to cry. I remember feeling so overwhelmed. I was petrified at the thought that we indeed did see this angel. The that hit me the hardest was that there was no way that we could have fabricated these events. The angel Peg had seen in the freezer had six wings and this Xeroxed paper told me his name was Raphael and the two sightings were joined on this paper. I wondered if we were both going to die having seen an angel. Never had anything like this ever happened to me and I began to think about how Raphael's instructions were to go to the priest and tell him that He was here. No one would believe us I deliberated and I was terrorized by the thought of telling anyone because that would make it even more real. Pride set in. I did not want to lose any credibility's I had gained thru the years.

I felt that Peg and I were **not** among the higher echelons in the Community and I was anxious about the idea of telling someone we had seen an angel much less have a name. After all who were we? I certainly was not going to tell my husband. We already had problems. After Peg and I settled down, and believe me it took awhile, she went home leaving us both with unanswered questions.

Prior to this Peg had made an upcoming appointment with Richard (the priest Raphael referred to) to talk about other issues. Peg and I were both having issues in our marriages, serious issues and often this brought us together to try to help each other. Peg decided that she would keep her appointment with Richard. At that point Peg and I were still in denial that things were as bad as they were in our marriages, both of us still thinking we could fix things somehow.

Peg decided to keep the appointment with Richard and also tell him about Raphael. It was for sure I was not going to tell him with having problems already existing in my marriage. The Thursday night before Peg's appointment with Richard we decided to come together to pray. We prayed hard that night and I can tell you that my prayer was, "Please let this cup pass by me." During this prayer I received this vision. I saw Raphael standing before a large group of mighty angels. Some among them seemed to me to be "warrior angels" while others seemed to be "in charge" angels. Raphael was reading to them from a parchment scroll. When he had finished I asked him in my mind what was on the scroll. He replied, "Instructions for journeys". There were names on the scroll that he said would be revealed later Just learning about Raphael's forte as being an angel of healing I suspected there were names there of people to be healed.

Some days later, before Peg's impending meeting, Raphael gave me a prophecy to take to Richard. I wrote it down. Raphael said that he would go before us and not to be afraid. Well, I was afraid and since Peg was going anyway, I just gave the prophecy to her to take with her. The Prophecy said, **"Do not be afraid, my name is Raphael and I am called:" Keeper of the Gates of the City". I have come to heal and to bind spirits.** There was also something about we would be sent as healers and messengers.

From second hand information about that meeting with Richard, Peg said the visit went like this. When Peg arrived Richard had been trying to make out-of- town reservations that week to go meet with his parents and could not find a room in a hotel in that town because there was some sort of convention going on. Just before Peg walked in he received a call that the rental people had been successful in locating a room for him at the Hotel Raphael. I do not recall the town we are talking about but I do remember the Hotel Raphael. Peg told Richard about our most recent events and gave Richard the prophecy I had been given. Richard got out this book in which a previous prophecy had been written 10 years before either Peg or I had even come to the

Community. This prophecy said that "an angel would be sent to the Community and He would call himself, "Keeper of the Gates of the City." This was the same identification as just written in the prophecy Peg had just handed Richard. We would have had no prior knowledge of this prophecy. Richard acknowledged and substantiate that what had transpired was genuine. He noted that all through the scriptures when an angel appeared his first words were, "Do not be afraid." The first two times he had appeared he used those same words. I wouldn't have known that either since I was not particularly scripture literate at that time. There was no doubt but that Raphael was here. After some time Richard put the prophecy in our local bulletin called, The Scroll. I had heard through the grapevine that there were others that also saw Raphael but I did not ask who, it was still sort of a shock for myself.

Healings Invoking Raphael's Name

Peg and I were at that time part of the healing team in the Community so we started invoking the name of Raphael as did the other healing teams. Powerful healings started to happen when Raphael's name was invoked. There was a young pregnant mother in the Community who was healed of cancer. She had a large tumor and it began shrinking and finally disappeared in amazement to her doctors before the baby was born. The doctors had previously wanted to terminate the pregnancy worried about the cancer and the fetus. The mother however took a leap of faith and said that she would not terminate the pregnancy.

There was a man who had trouble with his eyes but his eyes would not accept the corrective contact lenses and when prayed over in the name of Raphael his eyes accepted the contact lenses with no trouble. There were other healings.

A young boy born who had spinal bifida and when prayed over invoking Raphael's name the bone grew in place and when the bandages were removed not only was the missing bone in place but his back was completely healed. Today he still carries the scar of this healing where the open wound on his back healed leaving a long scar. There were other healings and by this time the others who had seen Raphael had started coming forward and invoking His name.

A Personal Message from Raphael

A message that needs to be told to every human being: I told Raphael how honored I was that He an angel was standing in front of me. I shall never forget his words, *"No, it is I who am privileged to meet you. We are created emissaries of God's mercy and love, you are the good news. We were created to serve you being the Children of God. You are the good news."* Again, I was flooded with emotion.

A Journey with Raphael - The Akashi Records

Raphael has taken me many places over the next few years during our many encounters. One of the places He took me

He called the **Room of the Akashic Records** (I have spelled like I heard it). As far as the eye could see on each side of me, upwards and downwards there were these very old books, books, books. He let me feel one of the books but I was not allowed to open it. I asked him what this place was and why all the books. He told me that these were the journals of people's lives from start to present. I was holding a book of someone's reincarnations. The records were kept according to Raphael of a person's lifetimes as directed by God. Raphael told me that sometimes God will give special permissions, to access this information in special circumstances. I had never heard of an Akashic record prior to this journey. I asked Him if a person could access their own record and He stated that not usually but information was granted and shared in dreams sometimes and used by our guardian angels, always with God's permission. He placed my book on my lap and asked if I would like to access it. I, in fear declined. It was years later that again the Akashic records were referenced by an article I was reading. I was startled that here was mention of these books by someone else and that they actually existed. When I had returned from that journey with Raphael I chose to ignore it because I was sure I had lost my mind and perhaps it was really only a dream.

But later a series of dreams occurred in perfect sequence that seems relevant to the existence of such a past life.

A Past Life? The series of 5 dreams followed all in a row over a period of 5 nights. I never connected these dreams with the

Akeshic records until recently. I will recount the dreams as follows:

Dream #1 - I was married to a good man who seemed to be a farmer or herdsman I will call him. We had two children, a 8-10 year old son and an infant daughter. We lived very simply in a place that was remote, arid and dry with a sandy landscape. We were enjoying a simple meal from the land on which we lived. We were happy. I was nursing the baby and the boy would help his father with the daily chores. Our clothes were woven from a rather course material I want to say the feel of burlap or something similar.

Dream #2 - We were enjoying an evening meal when my husband told me that there were rumors of war but that he did not think it would impact us because we were so remote. He wasn't worried but more curious about the news.

Dream #3 - One day during the heat of the day there rode up over a hill a group of what seemed to be soldiers. They explained that my husband's services were needed for the army and that he must come with them. My husband objected. They forcibly took him and our son, placed them on extra horses they had with them and rode off with all our cattle as well. I never saw him again.

Dream #4 - I could not stay and found out that other men and boys had been taken and so joined the other women and children and old men left behind packing up what we could and started out to find a place to live, half starving. My daughter was still an infant and so I bundled her up. I was having trouble feeding her because I was hungry and had little milk to offer. Along with the others we made it to what I will call a refugee camp and lived there for almost a year.

Dream #5 - One day the soldiers came and broke up the camp killing many of the women and children in an effort it seemed to irradiate us. I heard one of the soldiers say to kill as many children as they could because the children were the next generation and they did not want them to survive. There was mass running and screaming and we all scattered. I ran and ran and ran keeping my daughter close to me. Finally I could run no longer and came to this bombed out stone building that was only a shell and I went inside and laid next to a wall with no roof. I never had looked at my daughter with all the running and when I laid down and unwrapped her, she was dead. I was so sad but had no tears because there seemed no liquid left in my body. I pulled her close and as I laid there I noticed next to the wall across from me was a decomposing body of a woman lying there. I died there holding my dead daughter.

That was the end of the dreams. The experience seemed to confirm that indeed perhaps this really was a past lifetime because the details and order of dreams seemed to point directly to the reality of reincarnation. Perhaps this is the reason that this time around I am here reincarnated with so many children. I have always loved my life and have said that it was not a struggle raising these children but rather a dream come true. It seemed also related to a chart reading by an well known astrologer that I had come to have these children out of a sense of loss. You know it was one of those fun things you did out of curiosity This all now seems related. And so, I decided to take the question to Raphael.

When I asked Raphael about the reality of past lifetimes He point blank told me "Yes," and that the wisdom these struggles brought by one earthly life now became lessons we brought with us to the next life. Some lifetimes that seem to end in tragedy often appear as tragedies but are not in the whole scheme of reincarnation. He said that we always have the choice to come back or not. Being raised Catholic the whole subject of reincarnation was a no-no at the time and so I now wonder.

Reincarnation could be the reason we are not to judge anyone. Maybe the whole thing has to do with where they are in their journey of reincarnation. Maybe we don't understand because it is not the only life they or we have had. If we are all here for lessons as some think than why should we judge their lesson? It does seem that the higher minded people like the Buddha's, etc have an easier time not judging and believing in reincarnation.

The Throne Room of the "Christ"

In the company of Raphael, the Archangel, I have seen and witnessed, surrounding the throne upon which the "Christ" sits, **beings of praise** that were singing it seemed. Their singing was beyond earthly description as to its sound. Raphael noticed what I will call my own rapture and told me, "It was not their voice that made the music but rather the purity of who they were." I understood. Because of their immense purity, the sound of their song was inconceivable. They also had no eyes or eyelids but rather just deep dark holes and again Raphael told me that we humans **think** we see with our eyes but that there is so much more left out because we **do** have eyes which focus on a small amount of that which is around us and eyelids that just for a split second dissemble the picture before us limiting what we do see. Raphael said real seeing is a matter of the heart. Real seeing is believing.

The throne was made of gold and jewels and upon it sat a light so bright I could not look at it directly, I asked Raphael, who in fact it was that sat on the throne and he said "The Christ". (Now I might want to add here that I did not understand because I always used the term Jesus Christ and thought for sure there was some lack of understanding on my part). Raphael went on the explain that "The Christ" was not Jesus Christ as comprehended. I had previously never heard of "The Christ" apart from Jesus Christ. Raphael explained that Christ was not Jesus's last name and He was Jesus of "The Christ". I did not learn for months later about "The Christ".

Other Journeys

Raphael often took me on journeys, sometimes to foreign places where I miraculously understood the language and was able to communicate with the people. I felt invisible but to the people I was not. These often happened during the night but I have had such experiences during the day too. There were times that I found myself in a position of authority as if I were one among them, helping the people to advert tragedy and other times much as an observer.

Raphael took me many times to other places. They are too many to recount here but were lessons many times. I have included here in this book some of the major journeys. Some of the others were personal journeys and some were social journeys aimed at understanding the Great I Am.

Other Angelic Meetings
The Angels of Opportunity

Along in my journey, I received another message from a group of six angels calling themselves The Angels of Opportunity. I told Father Richard about these angels and at the time he just remained silent. A few days later, on the Feast Day of the Archangels (a Catholic feast day), the Community came together to pray. Richard revealed during his homily that there had been six areas within the Community of concern and felt that six Angels of Opportunity, were here to help the Community leaders resolve the six areas of concern. The correlation between six angels and six areas of renovation seemed relevant even though I had no prior knowledge these discussion were happening. Richard shared this information during the Feast Day celebration.

I must tell you a funny story surrounding this celebration. During the service I saw this angel come in and she was to take our prayers to God she told me. I asked where the other angels were and she said that there was "a celebration of sorts" going on in heaven honoring the Archangels and that she had been sent because it was Her day to administer to the Archangels and so was sort of filling in. She told me her name was Janiel. When I returned home I immediately looked up the name Janiel in my *Dictionary of Angels* book but there was no reference. The next day I mentioned this to a good friend of mine, Jerry. By this time the story had started coming out. It seems that he did a lot of research for me came back about a week later with information about his research. He stated that with the help of some librarian he had indeed found the name Janiel only once referenced and that this angel was identified as an angel *in charge of Tuesdays*. You guessed it, the Feast Day celebration had fallen on a Tuesday. It is funny though when you think about angels having celebrations.

After this time not only Raphael materialized but other angels. On occasion I had met Michael who was dense in energy and huge in stature. I had met Gabriel who was delicate in energy. Michael being a warrior and Gabriel a messenger had completely different energies about them. There have been others who intermingled in and out of my life in times of need. There have also been animal spirits that would make themselves known for direction and wisdom. I could be wrong and this is only a guess, but I would say that everything living has a spirit that communicates.

The Angel Raziel

The morning were always my most sacred time. My children all slept late in the mornings during summer affording me some quiet time. One day I was out on the porch as usual and up the sidewalk walked an angel and sat down beside me. He continued to come every morning for weeks. It was not Raphael and he/she gave me all kinds of lessons that I was instructed to write down. Their content ranged from healing methods to how things were managed in heaven. I did not know who He was initially. He told me He would divulge His name on the day of the last lesson. I wrote the lessons down as instructed. On the last day He told me his name was Raziel. I looked him up in a copy of "The Dictionary of Angels" by Gustav Davidson a book that I had recently purchased. After a brief genealogy the book went on to say, ["*In rabbinic lore, Raziel is the legendary author of the Book of the Angel Raziel (Sefer Raziel), "wherein all celestial and earthly knowledge is set down." The true author is unknown but he has commonly been identified as Eleazer of Worms or Isaac the Blind, by medieval writers. Legend has it that the angel Raziel handed his book to Adam, and that the other angels, out of envy, purloined the precious grimoire and cast it into the sea, whereas God ordered Rahab, primordial angel/demon of the deep, to fish it out and restore it to Adam- which Rahab obediently did."*] The account goes on to say that the book was given first to Enoch, then to Noah, then to Solomon. The book was then lost. The book was suppose to contain mysteries not even given to other angels. Noah was suppose to have received the dimensions of the ark in this book. There is rather continuing lengthily description of Raziel that follows in the book. I could not wonder if indeed I was writing excepts from that same book that had been lost. There were many lessons on healing and the order of the hierarchy of the angels. I had a feeling that my lessons were only a part of the secrets written in Raziel's book After my lessons were completed at Raziel's request I turned the written lessons over to the healing team in the community.

Today I only have a few notes that were written but I remembered the first lesson very well and I will share it with you. Some encounters with the angels over the years are extraordinary memories, things that happened that touched me powerfully These events changed my life in some way and were personal and meetings that I shall never forget. I wish to share the very first lesson by Raziel with you now as it is still fresh in my memory after all these years.

Lesson on How to Use Colors in Healing by the Angel Raziel

The lessons entailed the colors used on Earth in relation to their healing abilities. He noted that the Sun being yellow brought warmth and vision and when used in prayer would bring insight and light into rather dark situations that a person might be dealing with. The color of the sky was blue which brought forth a peaceful feeling and was to be used in praying against depression and hopelessness because it lifted. The color of grass which was green was to be used in prayers of regeneration both of the body and mind. The color of red was to be used to instill a feeling of warmth to someone who was feeling lost, afraid and feeling cold. Red was the color of a the warmth of a fire meant to bring warmth and comfort from the cold. The color white he instructed was the color to pray in when you were not sure exactly what color to use. At the time I did not know that the color white is really every color mixed together. I thought that this would be black and was surprised it was indeed the color white.

In using white light there was an incident when my youngest son Matthew fell down a flight of steps and seemed sort of unconscious and so I put my hands on his head and summoned the white light and I saw a fracture line that ran through the back of his head. Later this same line was confirmed by x-rays taken at the hospital. Then there were the combinations of colors but every color given had divine reference to healing. Watch what feeling that color instills and you will have the reason to pray in that color.

A NEW CHAPTER

(These lessons were given from a source I call God who has many names) The name given to me was <u>"The Great I Am in Whom There is No I Am Not"</u>

(When I reference "God" I reference the name given above)

GOD IS REAL: More real than we could even experience here on Earth. Here on earth we experience "real" measuring it up against "not real". It's not the whole picture of reality. There are worlds in between. If I have the eyes to see and I see something I can say it is real because I have the eyes to see. But what if I did not have eyes to see....would it be any less real?

ABOUT THE HEART OF GOD: There have been many many lessons and illuminations I will call them, as told to me from these angelic beings as well as from Jesus and My Father who has many many names but it was instructed me, for a time, to call Him, "**The Great I Am in Whom there is No I Am Not**."

Personal Witness: I had gone out to sit on my patio to say my prayers, having my journal in my hands and without warning, God took my hand literally and placed it on what could have only been His heart. This heart was PURE LOVE. There were no judgments, no rules for good behaviors, no disappointments, no earning it, no wants, no needs, and way beyond anything ever even experienced here when we try to describe love. I just sat out on the porch, just sitting there moved to tears of joy for hours and yet disbelief because **I never knew such love COULD even exist**. I sat there just being there in that moment moved to tears and a great sense of joy never before experienced.

As I sat there in complete bewilderment about the whole situation that had just happened I sought God's comfort. You have to remember I had never had anything like this ever happen to me before, not to this degree. I went into the house to grab some tissues still being overwhelmed. As I sat down there were three doves that flew down and came to rest on the porch wall about 3 feet from my chair. They looked at me and after a few minutes flew away. My question was, "What is Your message God?"

Then, almost immediately two sparrows came, one landing on the elongated bird feeder and the other on the same wall as the doves. The sparrow on the bird feeder took a seed in his beak and flew down to the one sitting on the wall and actually put the seed in the other's beak feeding him and then they both flew off together. The understanding and the experience of unconditional love that day went way beyond even the first moment when they put that new born baby in my arms. That is the closest I can come to description but even that is not enough or even close. I felt however, that the directive to my question was answered with the arrival of the two sparrows, one feeding the other. This is in part why I am doing this writing to let God's words feed us.

I AM HERE TO TELL YOU GOD TOUCHES YOU: If anyone of us ever could doubt that our life and our soul did not matter you are so so wrong. You could **never really** believe it even if you believed in it. If out of all these writings that are about to be put down, you would believe this one thing **everything you ever even dreamed of or wished for would fall to the wayside in total reverence of how well you are loved**. Please believe me I am not making this up. Open your heart and ask God to come in....give Him the invitation. He loves spending time with you. I know this because He loves spending time with me. God is accessible. God wants to walk with us. He will give you the answers that you have asked for. He will laugh with you and hold you when you are crying. He will cradle you in His arms and bring meaning and purpose to your pain. Never, never, never are you alone. He has thousands and thousands of angels and helpers here just for you.... He is the first one that named us.... and our name is "beloved." **Now how does that make you feel?** Just think if we could see it for ourselves and everyone else what a difference it would make in the world.

GOD IS CIRCULAR IN NATURE: I have looked for 15 years for something square that God created. There is nothing on this Earth that I can find. Everything exists within a circular or oval pattern. and when I asked about this the answer was that if it is eternity there is only flow and movement never the end, thus the circular. A square is man's invention. If we are ever in a corner it helps to realize that we put ourselves there and need only step out into "possibility" which is circular in nature. When I was in elementary school we learned about the three God heads of God. God the Father, God the Son and God the Holy Spirit. I learned about them then, but today they are a reality.

MY QUESTION TO GOD RELATED TO ALIENS: Just curious God are there what we call alien life forms?

God: Funny they ask me the same thing about you. There are other races and other realities that have evolved within the solar system as you know it and do not know it. Evolution is everywhere and also here on Earth. You are the biggest proof of evolution. Today you are not the same as you will be tomorrow. Even your human life patterns are involved in rotation and recycling. Of course there is only more. You call them aliens and I call then evolutions. Think about this....from the same set of parents come siblings all who are different. Even identical twins are different one from the other. It is already a fact that you can relate to (I have a set of twins, numbers 12 and 13 and I called them salt and pepper twins because they were so different). *There are unlimited possibilities within your own species. Why then would you think that other species are also non-existent.*

OUR FUTURE AS HUMANS: *God: The future....I cannot predict your future. You have your future in our hands. I can only be invited in to help you change the criteria by which you want to live. I can change circumstances with permission and invitation. I gave you free will so that you could reach for answers, your answers. You can invite me in and pray for the "highest good" which by the way, never harms another person. The "highest good" for one will never harm another because it never will be a judgment but rather it is an enticement to trust. To trust in things not seen nor fully understood with our limited reality*

ARE "WE" REALLY THE ONE DOING OUR LIFE: So this morning I really got in touch how we think we are doing our life but really God is doing our life and we are just reactions to putting it all together. God is always before us. He puts things together way ahead of our wants and needs and our ideas. He sends the opportunities and we think we are doing such a great job but really we are responding to His divine help. Like my grandson, my grandson's wife and child came to live with me due to financial troubles They had to leave their rented home because there was a fire and had the house was condemned. At the time my grandson was in school and his wife was working a waitress job which did not pay much. Through the months she got a job with a Family Therapy group (the job came to her if you can believe) and because she is where she is she is now helping other immediate family members to get the help they need. I started out helping my grandson, his wife and child and now several years later they are helping me out. God engineered this whole thing when I did not even know that I would need help.

Another example, I just got from vacation with very limited funds and another granddaughter out of the clear blue sky called upon my return and asked if I had enough groceries. I told her that I have enough even though I did not and she said no matter that tonight she was going shopping and was bringing over groceries. I had not even asked for groceries. Often I have found out that whereas I often start out helping another and then they turn around and help me long before I even know that I need help. So the gospel according to Sandra is keep reaching out to others that may need help with no expectations other than serving God is a good thing for you too. Not just because it comes back but for the realization that we are all in this together and you know that scripture that says where ever there are two of you there I am.....it's true (not that He is not there for one of us too).

THE FEAR OF OLD AGE: I have been increasingly anxious of late about how I will be when I get really old (part of this is denial that at 73 I am well on my way). I know that the first half of my life has been so blessed I do completely trust that you God, will be there in my elderly years also. There is still fear however from time to time in spite of everything I know about you God. The only thing that my friend who is going through the same thing and I have come up with is to recognize the fear, bring it to God and then let it go. There is no fear that lives in your heart God but help me with my own. That's all I can say.

God....what you fear is the lack of control you have over things. Don't worry I have been with you all along and I will be there in your future also. Thank you for sharing your fear with Me. You know that life happens every day. Be grateful today and live in that. You as humans always try to live in the future and sometimes you miss today. Put that away. You really do not know what any day will bring. Some are old and some are young when things happen. If I loved you so much on this side of life just think how much you will realize that I love you on the other side too. Acknowledge your fear, give it over and look at the gifts of today. You of all people know that and this is just a reminder. Just remind yourself and trust. I love you.

He then went on to tell me that life is a circle. It never ends really it just takes bends. He went on to show me that nothing created ever ends. Even our trash piles of today will become something different tomorrow and thus "no end".

GOD ALREADY KNOWS WHAT WE NEED BEFORE WE DO: Last summer I went on a vacation to Destin, Florida with several friends and daughters. We went in two separate cars. When we collected our GPS cords I thought that I had the right one to mine but I was wrong.

Tonight I went with my friend Carol to downtown Cincinnati to visit a friend and watch the fireworks. On the way to Carol's I plugged my GPS in and it would not charge. I called Lisa and I said that I thought she might have been about having the wrong cord because my GPS would not charge. I was terrified to drive downtown Cincinnati without my GPS because I was unfamiliar with downtown and a ballgame was in progress and I had never been to my friends house either. I knew it would take driving at night in unfamiliar territory, not knowing where we were going. Carol my friend that was going with me tonight was as equally concerned.

Now Lisa lives in Crittenton, Ky quite a distance from me. She said that she would drop it off but I needed it now. I told her I had to have it tonight and when she offered to bring it to me it would not be here in time her living over 50 miles away in a different state even. "No," she said I am right up by your house I was bringing some clothes up there for Sarah her daughter-in-law" to try on. Lisa was just getting off the highway right about where I had pulled over To make a long story short, we both pulled over at the same site and she was able to give me the cord and I went on my way. Lisa never comes to my house because she lives in another state even. I think is was not accidental that she arrived right where I was a mile from my house with the cord that I needed. I figured that God had seen all the circumstances before I even seen them and arranged the meeting just in time for me to go on. God goes before us always. I have experienced this type of co-incidence more than once in my life It helped me trust my needs and future to God even more than before. He is always sending me reminders of his faithfulness and caring in such manners. Thank you God.

GOD'S DISCERTATION ON ACCESSIBILITY: *GOD: Good morning Sandra.* **Let me speak to you about My accessibility: I am always accessible.** *You have been given the gift to see me additionally in yourself. If more people would see and know who they really are, in divinity, there would be no wars, no judgments, no violence one against the other or the Earth. There would be no poverty, either of the mind, body or spirit. There would be no need to be right or wrong. There would be no divisions among yourselves. You would not have to own things because everything would be yours too. I am love and what you felt that day* (referring to that experience on my porch of love) *was the real and total presence of My abiding love. Every child would be cherished....and you are all My children. That is reality. I shall always bless all those who you pray for. I shall bless your own life beyond the reality of being human. I at your invitation shall set things that are not right....right. Within real truth resides a place for non truth.*

(I am reminded of something my oldest son Michael said recently "there are really 3 truths, your truth, my truth and THE truth)

DO WE BELIEVE BECAUSE WE 'SEE' OR DO WE 'SEE' BECAUSE WE BELIEVE: *GOD: You have had a question all day long so let's talk about it.* **Your question is that if you do not see something does it really exist***? You question comes from a show you saw on television about this recorded underwater rescue of a woman in a submerged car. It shows the state of panic she was in while still above the water where the rescue fireman were unable to break any of the windows for her escape. A few minutes later the whole car sunk and was under water and it looked eminent that she would drown. During the underwater filming it showed the fireman going around the entire car still trying to break a window for her escape with no success. The rescue fireman eventually surfaced in the front of the submerged car, coming up for air. He suddenly saw her hand reaching out of the water and he pulled her to safety. They gave her mouth to mouth necessitation and she responded. It all looked like a normal rescue until they pulled the car out of the water and later realized that there were no broken or rolled down windows and yet she was able to reach out her hand to make contact with the rescuing fireman. The windshield did not exist for her because she was concentrating on the fireman and was able to go past the windshield. It is a good lesson on being careful where you put your concentrations.*

Do this experiment. Look forward and notice all that you see. Then turn around and see everything there that you can see and notice. Because you turned around does your first sighting cease to exist. Reality is really both views so as to your question about seeing, the answer is seeing always is experienced from the place you stand but there is always so much more that is not seen everywhere. That's why I ask you to believe because it does not have limitations to seeing only what you are able to perceive.

PRAYER - GOD'S LOVE: A good friend of mine suffered a heart attack while we were camping. She died that day and the expertise of the paramedics, doctors and the prayers of many friends and family and God's love of her that brought her back. She says the experience changed her relationship to her Creator. While she was between worlds she witnessed that the only solitary thing she could hear were all the prayers of the people. She came back with very limited memory of anything but the prayers.

Because of her near death experience and her ability to hear only the prayers, she has developed a new perspective on the importance of prayer. She also has a deeper realization of the power that prayer and how it makes a real difference. She herself having no real control over her destiny while in a coma, feels that her destiny was decided by those praying for her. At this point I might add that she heard the prayers in all different languages. After prayer I realized that some of the people had different experiences of their God. Some praying was done in the Buddhist tradition, some in the Native American traditions, etc. I am wondering if that wasn't witness to God has many names but is the same God and done according to the intention of the prayer. That insight she came away with was directly related to the power of prayer not a specific prayer of just one modality.

A QUESTION ABOUT WALK-INS: OK this morning I woke up and got my cup of coffee and after that was finished I came into the computer and accidentally pulled up this site called "healyourlife.com". For some reason I clicked on an article talking about the possibility of walk-ins and it resonated because I had such an experience when I was at New Jerusalem Community. The experience: The night before a friend happened to stop by that had been gone over a year and had joined this community (later to find out that it was a cult) out West and when she was talking all of a sudden I felt myself being drawn into her eyes and it frightened me and when I turned around, the kitchen in which we were sitting was getting smaller and smaller as if I were in some sort of tube and was being drawn further and further away. I called on Jesus and almost instantly I was back in the kitchen. I did not share this with her and she left. The next morning I got up and was deathly sick. I felt I was going to pass out and so from the bottom of the steps I called for my husband who came to the top of the steps and came down and immediately started praying with me. Honest to God I could feel this thing walk in and out of me. As soon as he would pray it would walk out and when he stopped it would walk back in and I would be sick. My husband called the priest Father Richard Rohr the pastor of our community and he immediately sent a good friend of our's over who was a counselor of some sort and she said some prayers and the thing left. Richard came over and gave me Eucharist and gave me some to keep at home and take each morning. I did as he instructed and the thing never came back. I asked him why me and he said that I was so open that I was like a tree with no bark and I needed to learn about protecting myself and told me to find out about the gift of Discernment, which I did. My husband said that the reason he came running down the steps was because where my eyes had been were black holes and steam was coming out of them. It scared him too.

Ok when I read the article about walk-in's. The article went on to say that at birth often we give permission for another spirit to co-habitate with us in our body. This spirit or soul is from God because we just came from God and the agreement is that they who are enlightened can work thru us and thus share our body. I did not know nor do still not really know if this is possible

So on reading this article I thought that perhaps it was very possible. With that a good friend of mine called and told me that she did not know what was going on with her that morning but she was completely falling apart, could not remember things, things were not where they were suppose to be, etc. The more she talked the more there seemed to be a relationship to what just had happened to me about these walkins. I wondered if that was not what was happening to her and told her about what I was reading. After we finished our conversation and she hung up I again went back to the computer. All of a sudden there was this, I will call it a directive that said look at the word "your." The directive said you know that **"your"** is a word understood by you as something that belongs to you. But take another look at "your" do you not see two words? Look, there is "you" and "our". My question still is unresolved in my own mind but maybe it is possible to share your soul as with everything else.

QUESTION ABOUT HOW TO CARRY PAIN: Good morning God. This morning my heart is heavy with sadness. I am sad for so many people and myself included. The one thing I did not think of was the incredible amount of pain that went along with being your servant. How do you carry this Lord? How do you deal with it and more importantly how do I carry this pain. I know about the light and your grace. I know that you always are a good and loving father but I still feel the pain of so many in so much pain. I know my heart won't break because I have you Lord but it sure doesn't feel good. What do you have to tell me about all this Lord.

God: You are in pain because you are still human. Yes, you know that divinity exist within you but pain of being human is real. But, that is what causes each and every person to reach out. Pain always causes you to reach out to Me but remember it is not always what comes together but also what falls apart. If things did not fall apart things would not come together either. It is what you hold on to that causes you pain. You have to put things in the right balance. Every failure is an opportunity for success. Some take it some do not. All you can do is put light there even though you are not feeling light. Remember Jesus died for your pain also. Let the feeling come and go because these are only your reactions to what is taking place and you do not have the whole answer. It is by grace that you can even feel pain. As I have told you just live 24 hrs at a time not trying to put it all together. Often what you want for another is not the "highest good". Bring yourself to Me. Ask that I help you deal with the pains and disappointments and devastations that you see around you. Know that I am God and and so in part are you. Live in expectation of that. Without sadness you would not experience joy. Minimize the sadness and maximize the joy. Remember when my children were in the desert and I fed them everyday just for the day. That's what I do and that's where I am. Don't look to tomorrow only to today. I am here and I am always here even when you cannot see or feel me. You wanted the whole picture and here it is.

A CONVERSATION ABOUT WORRY: Sandy: I am going to witness to something that has really helped me deal with the many worries I have and believe me with this big family I have plenty along with my own about me. This was bothering me one night when I really felt swamped. I went to God for a solution not believing one was possible except for me to stop worrying...and I had tried to stop in all kinds of ways. Ok when I went to God here were the instructions,

God: Sandra do you remember that scripture that talks about when the apostles and I were out on a lake one night and a terrible storm came up and the apostles feared for their lives (Matthew 9:23-27). Remember I was sleeping in the boat and they woke me up to ask my help. Remember what I told them....I am here in the boat so why do you find it necessary to wake me up if I am here with you. How can you be afraid if I am here? Ok Sandra look around the room and find a boat.

Sandy: A boat, I thought but looked around and sure enough there was a little canoe sitting on one of my dressers so I grabbed it and asked if that would be OK. The answer was yes that this would be fine

God: OK now get some resemblance of Me and put it in the boat.

Sandy: Well I looked and looked around for a medal with God on it or a picture of Jesus or something that could do this I could not find anything that I thought appropriate. Then God asked me if I saw that little statue sitting on my dresser also and when I said yes He directed me to get it. I questioned His choice because it was a Native American mother on her knees with lots of children playing on her back and all around her (I have Native American roots and lots of children so I thought it appropriate for me but not for Jesus but did as directed anyway).

He instructed me to put that in the boat and I followed His orders and it just fit in the canoe. Then He directed me to get a piece of paper and tear it up into little pieces big enough to write a name on it. I did so. He then directed me to sit down for a minute and write the name on a piece of that paper of anyone I was concerned about. After contemplation I had about 8 pieces of paper with the names on. Then He charged me to fold the pieces of paper and put each one in the canoe which I did. Then He said....

God: Now Sandra remember the story about the apostles. Well here are the names of those you worry about just like the apostles were worried about when they had Me in the boat. Don't you

wake Me up either ....simply put the names in the boat and walk away worry free. I AM IN THE BOAT. DO NOT KEEP PETITIONING ME FOR THEIR SAFE KEEPING THEY ARE IN THE BOAT WITH ME AND JUST LIKE I HAD INSTRUCTED THE APOSTLES DO NOT WORRY.

Sandy: Well I have used that boat for over a year now and there **has not been one concern or person I have put in that boat that has not been blessed.** I above all others are also blessed because today I am able to also put people I care about and prayers have always been answered without worry and often resolutions never thought about. So now every couple of weeks I take a look at the papers in the boat and I take the ones out that are of no more concern to me and I put the papers in what I call a "thank you for answered prayers" jar. It is getting very full and I continue to put my concerns in the best hands possible. Thank you again God. I have often thought about the Native American woman with the children on her back used to represent Jesus. I figured it is about a mutual admiration relationship so don't be surprised about what He tells you to put in your boat to represent Him if you decide to make your own.

Just recently there came a further instruction regarding the boat. Every night I am to put in the boat with prayer, my concerns. Then in the morning I am to empty the boat, not looking at the slips of paper but rather disposing of them. I am to hold the empty boat and then return it to my fireplace mantle. I am to begin a new day, this day, not taking the concerns of the previous day with me....because today will not be a new day if I carry the concerns of the prior days and I will miss the newness in this day ahead. I get the image of an empty vase and have heard somewhere that the value of a vase is in the empty space inside. If the vase is filled than there will be no room inside.

MY WITNESS: RIGHT ORDER: In the Native American culture there is a way they eat that says something about who they are. The children eat first, they are the future, the elderly next, they are the wisdom, the working class third, they are the strength and THE CHIEF EATS LAST because he is the servant of the whole tribe and has the responsibility to look after all of them.

God: *All of what you have put down is the basic truth on how you are all to live. You will notice that there is purpose to each age group but a wise man will remember that I said that the first shall last and last shall be first in the kingdom. So tell all of those you know who strive to be servant's to the rest, to celebrate who they are for one day they will be sitting next to ME.*

MY QUESTION ABOUT GOVERNMENTS: God why is everything such a mess with the government, people's lives, and relationships?

God*: Because you are living in a time of renewal. As you well know things are really getting out of hand and away from the source from which they were created. The systems that are failing are part of this renewal. Stay close to ME and the values on which were placed My love The problem is that the letter of the laws have become the criteria instead of the heart of the laws* *from which they were created. Government has replaced, in many people's lives the criteria that came from the heart More and more the true meaning of democracy as you call it has been irradiated, and only used as a "token" title. How can things be alright and still have an increase in violence one toward another. There are too many measures. You are being dictated to from outside sources rather than from inside your hearts. You will notice that when something happens humanitarianly it makes the news. That is because it is rare and therefore is published. Take time each day to make a good difference. Even the approaches used to change things are often violent. Do no harm one to help another. Live in peace and harmony not in unrest and separation. I never asked anyone to change another thru violence, only love and prayer. A person is not capable to change things for the better becoming dominant. You will notice in the Scriptures those who I have made dominant were servants to the people. Often those who say they are serving are only serving themselves. Take notice of the things that are not working and pray for this renewal upon which I have My hands, Don't try so much as to make the change but rather be the change, I love you.*

MY QUESTION; ARE OUR WANTS AND NEEDS IMPORTANT? *God: Please do not think that I do not care about your want. I do and more. So do not be afraid to ask for something and just like your earthly father I can say yes or no but trust that the no is really another yes only further down the line. But, it gives me great pleasure to give to you make no mistake about that. And, because I give to one does not mean that I cannot give to another. That's sometimes your mistake to*

think there is only so much to give and that's not true. It was told to you once that you think of yourself standing in line 8 deep for presents and when you count the presents you see only 7 so you surrender your right to have one in lieu of taking something from another. First I am the giver of all and do not consider lack. So always ask. I want you to ask. I want you to trust. I want you to know how much I love you and how you make me even laugh sometimes. I love you.

MY QUESTION REGARDING SICKNESS: God there are many questions I have right now about all the things going on with everyone. There is much sickness and big issues going on with so many. Is there anything that I can do with all this.

God: Trust Me and put them in the boat.

MY WITNESS: MY PLACE: God there are many teachings about what we call "my place" being the place inside to go when stress and anxiety seem to appear and take over. So, I thought about my place and it is a place on a cliff that overlooks a river in the Fall of the year with all the brightly colored trees all around. Where you can feel the soft wind and hear only the sounds of nature. Where there is no human activity but only the earth and the animals, the flowers, the trees and the sound of the rushing water below. It is a place where everything dances in the wind and the rain and which sleeps and rises in the morning to the sun and retires at night with the moon. A place so still that you can hear your heart beating with no other sound.

Meditation
My Place

It is a place of the heart
Where there is.... no mind
And you're FREE to start
Casting off that which binds

Where the shafts of light
Reach down to your soul
And you exhale out of sight
The thoughts that control

And you learn presently... to be
Just You and Me

by Sandra Orlando

*God to Me: Ok I know that you have been going through a lot with so many around you going through crises after crises. I appreciate you praying for them and yourself too and I know that you love these people. I love them too. Take this to your earthly grave with you, HOW COULD GOD POSSIBLY LIE ABOUT CARING? I cannot lie and you do not have to always second guess your prayers or your motives or am I being selfish, etc, etc, etc. I AM HERE and I love you and I know the desires and the pains of your heart. Know also that I am NOT FRAGILE and you do not have to **not** level with me about doing or saying the right thing. Our wills are the same but sometimes the paths are different but still the same path. What about, "Thy will be*

Done." Isn't that the highest place to be? You are right, when you pray for that person's highest good, you are giving it over to me and that WILL NEVER be a disappointment for that person you are praying for. Yes you get scared and yes you get sad and yes you cry or get angry. I do not look upon that as a weakness it comes from a strength of the heart inside you. You do not have to be strong to have Me love you. It's OK to ask, it is OK to be scared, it is OK to be angry. Do you think I walk away from you ever? I do not ever. I am always with you and with the one's you are praying for too. I cannot be anywhere else, It is the "Our Father" in action. Note in this time of the year Fall, the trees do not groan and moan losing their leaves because I have seemingly deserted them. Nature has many lessons to help you on all your paths. It is something tangible, something real to you, something to understand with. But know above all else, "Yes, I do listen."

MY WITNESS: I HAVE A LONG WAY TO GO: Today I looked at a child on facebook who was starving. I felt very bad and then I felt good because in my life I have fed starving people through organizations like World Vision, etc.

So I was feeling pretty good that I had made a difference in my life feeding the poor and thanked God for the opportunity to do so. Then.....I realized I had nothing to be thankful about.....except that I was not the one being fed. And, I asked myself how much greater is this child than myself in the eyes of God. How dare I pat myself on the back for making a difference sharing out of my **extras** when this poor child has nothing to share. Oh my God I have a long way to go. When you say, blessed are the poor I think you were talking about me because I know that in your kingdom this child would never starve. I better get in touch with not being so proud at his expense.....

Lately God has instructed me to think of two words. One is arrogance and the other integrity. It is arrogance to level judgment against another who has come from a place that you have not been. You can only really understand hunger when you yourself have been hungry. Be grateful instead that you have not been hungry. The other word, integrity is about where would you be today if not for the gifts given you.... realize that everything is gift and use them wisely, not looking at them as something you deserve. Use your gifts with honor.

MY WITNESS: Things have been really rough lately. So many people close to me are dying or very sick. My own 96 year old father is in turmoil first at the hospital, then at a nursing home, then at the hospital and today at a different nursing home. My sisters and I have had care of him at his own home for about 4 years and have between the three of us been able to care for him and his needs. My sisters have been much more involved with him then I have but I have done what I could given my large family commitments and age. I have however done what I could do and have in many ways compromised my own life to take care of his. He fell and broke his hip, was operated on but struggles with the aftermath as far as physical. My youngest sister also cares for her husband's mother who is in a nursing home and suffers from dementia as well as her own family members. My other sister who also cares for him has just received news that her husband has to have a very serious operation that could greatly compromise their lifestyle. In my own family there has been much discord and sickness and accidents, etc. It seems that everyone around us requires serious prayers for serious issues. Even though I am surrounded by family and good good friends I have often felt so alone in dealing with all these issues. It has caused great tension and some depression even though I know that God cares and mentally I trust Him with everything. But, it still does not take the struggles away.

I was feeling so alone last night, so stressed, so anxious that I think it was making me physically sick. I know better but I still felt this way, alone. Then something happened and instead of knowing God was there, I FELT that God was there. The tiredness lifted, the anxiety and fear lifted, the hopelessness lifted. For the first time in a long time I KNEW God, that you were there. I FELT it and I was able to "not be alone" in these struggles. It was like everything was going to be OK. I realized the difference between knowing and feeling. Knowing lives in the head and feeling lives in the heart. Knowing tries to put all the scenarios together but feeling lives just for today, with trust in You by my side. It was a gift you gave me I am sure and now I really really know that I am never alone and that you are with me wherever I am. I do not think that I shall ever feel alone again. Thank you for this realization for I am sure it has changed my life. Do you have anything to tell me God this day.

God: Live each day as the only day, close by my side and in friendship, trust and love. That is who I really am. Not some

concept or solution or savior. Things are going to happen and I am
close. I am God and you are my child. I shall always be there....
always. You are never alone. Try not to figure out everyone else's
life but strengthen your own with this knowledge so that I may
send you anywhere in any situation and you shall not fear. Take
each day as it comes sometimes with laughter, sometimes with
tears, sometimes with stresses and sometimes with thanksgiving
but know you are never alone and tomorrow will always be
different than today. So therefore, take one day at a time

I could go into many examples of this in my own life but they are personal and it would be very detrimental at this time to name people, places or things. Seeing and understanding this teaches me to look inside myself first, instead of outside myself, to see what is going on. I realized that in judging another I first have to have **recognition** of the judgment **within myself** and so I have to ask myself, "Do you make this judgment out of my own personal needs or wants? Then I examine my own life. That does not mean that I automatically cancel my concerns or observations but it does make me mindful of my part of my decision. I realize that you cannot live life without making judgments but I have noticed that it has made me answer to things in my own life that I can change too. Because I see so many in need of the things that I automatically have, makes me re-examine the use of things I take for granted. I have seen some rich people be really poor in ways, and I have seen some people that are poor be really rich in my judgments of what is really important. I have come to see however, that what is important to me in not necessarily important to another and I am a whole lot less judgmental as to the actions of another realizing that the values acted on are different but interestingly enough. I have accepted myself for who I am and what I value in life giving the same space to others. My perceptions of what is perceived are mine and are only a part of wanting to make a difference....there are others also wanting to make a difference with their perceptions and we can learn from each other if we take the time to really listen without first judging or writing them off. It makes for a much larger world.....

A WINTER'S MORNING REFLEXTION: Good morning God. It is cold and snowy and icy out there and I am so grateful that I have a warm home, food, shelter and the time with You. Jason, my son, called this morning and we had a very good conversation about You Lord. You know Lord how I have had this struggle about realizing that the Bible we have in our hands today is not the total truth and how it was scrutinized by scholars thru the ages with things being removed and even how certain books were omitted and incomplete versus given us. It has been a struggle for me to read this book with all the changes that man engineered and so has left me with lots of doubt and misinformation about the whole truth given to mankind.

God: Your dedication is well received. I ask also that you consider three sources of information. 1) the earth and it's wisdom, 2) the scriptures and 3rd, trust in the grace I send to understand and keep true to the path of Love.

Sandy: I heard of quote today that made me laugh: Blessed are the cracked for they let in more of the light. Think about it....

if this isn't right? It has always been about salvation anyway right? It feels good to be cracked huh?

Sandy: There is another one that always makes me laugh: Don't let life get you down. Remember even Moses started out as a basket case!!!!

MY WITNESS: Good morning God thanks for waking me up today. Lately I have been waking up to the phone or to worry about someone else or the schedule for today and so I am trying to think up of another way to wake up. Here is my idea God. I want you to wake me up. It is the start of a day you gave me anyway and so I think it appropriate. I cannot think of a better way to be awaken than by someone who loves me like you do anyway. So any thoughts God?

God: It is always important that you ask Me into your day ahead. It is the gift of being child-like.. Children usually want to go out and play even if it is raining. Not so much by adults. But children, they love it even when the sun is not shining.

Sandy: It was Thanksgiving Day and I was at a family gathering. There were lots of people and lots of food. I was not particularly thinking about anything or anyone, just standing in the crowded room in the food line and all of a sudden this warm, loving presence came over me and surrounded me with no invitation at all. I turned and looked behind me and there was standing a family member who I never understood and seemed to go against everything I thought to be loving and I have had serious issues with for a long time. All of a sudden I felt this love from the feeling that swept over me and I went up and embraced him with a hug that was so genuine and real and full of love I almost wanted to cry. This feeling did not come from inside me but from the outside in. I never thought there would be a day when I thought I could say to this person, "I love you," but it was happening. God was that you because it sure wasn' t me. Can you help me explain this whole experience to myself?

God: Yes of course that was me. I am always love both within you and outside you. I just looked down and saw him standing there and used you to show him, or should I say let him feel, my love for him. It was my presence that always fills love and filled it that day. Even though you were not consciously aware of My presence there, I was there. I used you and do all the time to show love and affection. My love is a perfect love and knows no boundaries of time or space. Love always fills, always.

Well children it is the end of another one of your years. It has been good to see so many manger sets in your homes. This is the never ending story of your lives on Earth. There will be many changes this coming year and they will not all be easy or welcomed at first.

CHRISTMAS, DECEMBER 25, 2013: Happy birthday Jesus. Thank you for coming for us. Thank you. God, I have a question. My son is driving across the State of Michigan in terrible terrible snow and ice and is about 75 miles from home. I petitioned you for his safety and I am going to fast from smoking that last cigarette before I say my prayers and go to bed. In the past I have always talked myself out of doing fasting, feeling like it never really made a difference. I never really knew if fasting made any kind of difference. Tell me about fasting Lord because I really don't know or understand the "why?" of it.

*God: What fasting does is put "intention" to your request. Over the years I have asked for certain peoples at certain times to fast because I wanted them to clear their own agenda's to bring clarity. Did you even notice how selective and purposeful intention makes an unspecified inspiration. It is not done **so that I hear you** but rather it is done so as to create a clearing. A clearing in the forest is....a space without trees in an area of land that is wooded or overgrown. Fasting sets up a clearing in your spirit the same way as in the forest.*

Sandy: OK God I have a question for You and I do not want to seem pushy or anything but could You please help me....I don't know if this is something that has come to mind because You are talking to me or it is just my curiosity. Here is the event. It is terrible weather here right now and there is ice all over the place and record colds, below zero. It is very dangerous to be out tonight and I woke up at a little after 4 a.m. and had the urgency to pray for all those on the road, my family, if any of them were out and everyone around them also on the road. I went back to sleep thereafter. This morning I woke up and found out thru a communication that my youngest son, Matt, was indeed on the road because there was a foreign student living with his family that is from China and Kelly (the student) was coming back from Christmas break in China and arriving at Cleveland, Ohio with a connecting flight that was suppose to bring her to

Cincinnati where we live. It seems the flight was cancelled so Matt drove up to Cleveland in the dark in weather worse than we were having here. I did not know anything about his trip till this morning when I saw his posting on facebook. I called him to see what was going on and he was on his way home with Kelly, the student. I prayed for the rest of his journey home, for his safe return and he is now home. I texted Matt to see what time he left and it was on or near the time I woke up. My question is do You, the Almighty work thru us humans in such a way that needs our involvement? When I was reflecting on the Scriptures I noticed that all great and wonderful actions in which You participated always involved some human involvement. Is that to give witness? Could you tell me what is going on with this or is it just me?

God: Anytime you pray you are putting yourself in My presence. I do not need your presence all the time as you might think but anytime you put yourself in My presence in prayer know that I hear you. If I hear you I have an invitation upon which to act. But along with that, who do you think it was that woke you up in the first place. Yes, it is called solidarity. The words in your thesaurus further identifies it as unity, harmony, cohesion, shared aims, commonality. A prayer from the heart is always in solidarity.

PERSONAL WITNESS: OK HERE IS A FUNNY LITTLE PERSONAL EXPERIENCE I HAD ABOUT GOD TO INTERRUPT ALL THIS SERIOUS STUFF.....THINK ABOUT IT.

Last night at some point, I found myself far....far.... from our Universe witnessing many star and planet systems apart from what I recognized as our Universe. I was in awe of a much, much bigger construction of the reality of space and was taken back by just how big and vast was universe after universe. It was truly beautiful. I have no recollection of anyone traveling with me or even if there was a journey made. I cannot even to this minute reconcile myself with the infinite total of space. When I returned it left me with the emptiest feeling that I was but just a speck of dust by comparison. I came back feeling so insignificant and so meaningless in a universe so immense. I thought how can I even believe that I matter? How can I believe that God sits here and talks to me? How can I believe that I am of any importance at all being this tiny speck in such a vastness? Then I heard God's voice again.

God answered: *God said I was absorbed into forever. We really have no idea about forever. It was beyond even my imagination, There are no words no concepts to describe it. No wonder I felt like a piece of dust.* **Then God went on to explain it even more** *"Yes I know your uncertainty so by comparison let me direct your thoughts to a children's book entitled "Horton Hears a Who". Let me give you some similarities by which to understand. First, let me take you to Horton, the elephant. Elephants are known to have superior hearing abilities. The story is about an elephant who kept hearing this tiny little voice and finally traced it to the head of a clover. He plucked the clover and carried it about on the end of his trunk..Finally the voice identified itself as a Who. The story goes on to describe that on the end of this clover there existed a tiny town called "Whoville"* *where many whos lived. Imagine how Horton the elephant could hear that tiny voice from a wee little Who. Think about Whoville being a extensive town. All the Horton's friends made fun of Horton who very diligently cared for this clover. Then the story goes he lost the clover in an enormous clover patch (the universe). He was so upset that he searched and searched and finally found the clover again,(how many times have I had to come find you again). Reflect on how Horton (Me) was yet able to find that particular clover (your planet Earth) hearing that minuscule little voice (you). Think about how he held it high in the air with the tip of his trunk and established an ongoing relationship with this seemingly being no larger than piece of dust (as you felt). Can you begin to see the analogies?*

Sandy: That God has such a sense of humor, it never ceases to amaze me that He likes to laugh. The comparisons made me laugh.

A couple of days have now passed and I have been trying to articulate the experience trying to further explain it with no language suitable. The closest I have come is that it was not about a journey of the spirit, it was more that **I felt absorbed into Forever** as stated. It was as if I was standing in the Great I Am. That is as close as I can come to understanding or trying to articulate the why, what and where I existed within the presence. We really do not have any idea here on Earth of forever. It is beyond any sense of measure known to mankind.

God: So you may ask about yourself why you? Because you have been especially diligent in our journey. Is there anything that you do that you do not ask and invite Me into? That's why you hear Me so plainly I always have an invitation. I invite everyone to use prayer as a means of connection to Me but you are a prayer. I know that you still have trouble believing that but it is true.

I look at the planet and see what I have created being abused and misused and misappropriated in so many ways. Even your brothers and sisters, the animals are dying out from this great abuse. The way you live is the way you think. Reexamine the things you do and decide if you need to change it and then act on it and it will change your thinking. Don't look for miracles outside yourself but rather accept that each one of you is already a miracle.

HOLDING WITNESS: *Remember we talked about the terrible storm that shook the earth after My Son was crucified. Remember I told you that the storm was My witness that what happened was not right. Well sometimes it is a call for each and every one of you to be a storm also as in the case of crises.*

TO HEAL you must be willing to be present as My advocate of love. You must be willing to listen with that "pure heart" you felt that day I came - My heart. You walk with more wisdom now because I have sent you those who walk beside you, the angels, who teach you My way's wisdom.

WHERE IS MY DARKNESS LORD? *If you do not know where it is, it does not exist. You know that there is darkness but you also believe in the light more than darkness and so it does not exist. For you there is only illumination. It's about making your light brighter. When it is brighter it has the ability to reach* *more darkness. Someday there will only be light and you must help that along. That is why I tell you never to turn your face from Love. Because you have touched My Heart you know what it is, Love. Use it.*

I send you some discerning ways:

If the leader is last to receive - follow him/her
If when you eat you give thanksgiving - trust it will nourish you
If one professes his gratitude with action - trust him
If one goes an extra mile - trust he/she knows me
If one gives honor even to those who seem to have no honor - trust he/she is honorable
If one gives out of his own need - trust he/she will be provided for
If one has tears in his eyes - trust his/her heart
If one pray silently without acclaim - trust the source
If one can sit with you in your grief - there is a true friend
If one judges not - he/she will be given compassion

A WITNESS TO TIME GAPS: Some years ago my friend Mickie and I went on a trip out West and one day we were lost on an Indian Reservation. We had driven for miles without seeing anyone and I mean we were completely lost and our GPS was not working on the reservation. All of a sudden we came upon two tables where two Indian women were sitting, in the middle of nowhere and on these tables they were selling Native American jewelry. We pulled over because one, we were lost and two it was a most peculiar site in the middle of nowhere. As I stepped out of the car and my feet hit the ground it was like I was standing in the middle of a movie.

I saw coming over the hill in front of us, US Calvary riding many horses and they swooped down upon a population of Indian women and children and old men chasing them over the hill off to my right. They were shooting the Indians and out of the whole scene I was drawn to watching a young Indian girl I would say around 4 or 5 that the mother was pulling by the arm trying to get her and the child over the hill. At one point the little girl, holding a corn husk doll turned toward me, still running and just looked at me. It was like she knew me or something. Then the mother and the little girl ran toward the hill and the incident was over. I was crying at this point and when the two women at the table saw I was crying they approached me and asked what was the matter. I told them the scene I had just witnessed. They told me that I was standing on the very spot where an Indian massacre had happened and that the hill I pointed to was the very hill where one of these women's great grandfather had been killed by the soldiers. We were standing on the very site of Wounded Knee. She confirmed that over the hill was where the soldiers killed all the women and children and old men, one of them being her grandfather. In fact they pointed over another hill on my left and said there was the graveyard where they were buried. The woman said that what I had seen was exactly what happened as she was told by her elders. My friend Mickie and I went up the hill and visited the graveyard. It was in poor condition and instead of concrete markers there were often wooden crosses with names on them. We would have had no knowledge of this place since it was our first trip out West. The whole incident left me with the little girl looking at me like she knew who I was. I can picture her to this day. It was like I was standing in a movie all except for her.

Years later after this incident Ashley as a young adult granddaughter came back into my life. We had common threads between us which seemed to have no logical answers. One was our common love of the Native Americans and this sense that we were connected somehow to each other. The thought crossed my mind that maybe, just maybe, she was that little girl looking back. I have no proof but only a very strong feeling.

QUESTION: WHY ARE WE HERE? We are here to experience Choice - real choice but I can tell you it is usually only based on what we already know. When I asked the "Great I Am in Whom There is No I Am Not" it was whispered in my ear,

God: Because I love you and to really know Me your Father and Creator you must know and learn who I am not. I give you humans the ability to create with the freedom of choice. When you left the garden it broke My heart, the first children deciding to leave. That's why you are here, to know, love and serve Me in the complete knowledge of who I am. It is a journey you make through yes and no. I love you that much to again give you choice.

I look at the planet and I see what I have created being misused in so many destructive ways. Even your brothers and sisters, the animals are dying out from this great abuse. The way you live is the way you think and vice versa. Re-examine the things you do and decide if you need to change anything. Then act on it and it will change. Don't look for miracles outside yourself.....each one of you IS a miracle

Written Upon My Father's funeral mass reflection February 21, 2014 (He was 96 years of age)

A reflection comes from something real. My dad was real for 73 years of my life and therefore many reflections belong to both of us. He was there my whole life and my life mattered to him. It mattered when I cried. It mattered when I laughed. It mattered to give me food, shelter, clothing and education in my early years. It mattered to him to in later years that I was happy and safe and well. His family always mattered. The reflection of my life always included him being there. I never doubted that he would not be.

He is not coming back here now and I will miss him ....but I will always hold him in my heart and know he is in every breath I take because he gave me breath in the beginning and now even beyond. That you for the gift of life dad, may I carry it well in memory of our reflections. Peace and Amen (it is done)

Today is a day after my dad's funeral. All night I dreamed of losing things, like my purse, my keys, etc. I think this is all related to losing my father and the impending fear of death for myself. I realized that I was afraid of death and then God spoke:

You of all people Sandy knows that there is no death, only ascension. Yes your body gives way but you know that you are not your body alone. It is your spirit that gives life to your body and that is what is real. There is no death only ascension. And that vastness you felt out in the Universe was an example of ascension. Remember that I am always with you so be not afraid. You had a taste of what forever looks and feels like. So live in the promise of tomorrow, however is comes and in whatever form because it will always be there. The feeling on Earth called love is close to it, You do not stop loving someone because they change. Neither do I. Because I love you there is change. Always rejoice and be glad for this is the day the Lord has made....always and forever to infinity and beyond (as the superhero's say). By the way that was a good analogy you used when explaining to your granddaughter what happens when you die. The part about looking at the toaster as something real but it really was the electric cord connected to the plug that allowed the toaster to work. Good job in describing the toaster as body and the electricity as spirit.

WHY DOES DEATH COME GOD TO PEOPLE WHEN IT DOES?

Sandy: Just a week ago there was an accident taking a young father. My son-in-law works for Duke energy and was injured on the job and has been off duty for several months now. He is a lineman and this often requires climbing poles to reestablish power, etc for Duke Energy. Because he has been off this young father who is my son-in-laws friend was taking his place that day when a pole he and a co-worker were climbing and the pole snapped in half and to make a long story short, my son-in-law's friend was killed in the accident. The funeral was very very sad because several months before this that family had lost their 7 year old son, who was a twin, in his sleep. It is a very sad time for all concerned. Meanwhile Raphael the Archangel has been around for the last three weeks and so I asked him why? Why did the son die and now why the father? I did not expect an answer it was more like a question in my mind but Raphael did respond and tell me this.

Raphael: The body is not real without spirit. Spirit is what is real and the body only a vessel for its habitation. The why of why things happen (the reason) rests in the world of the spirit. The body does not hold these answers and because it is constructed of the Earth is a temporary vessel predetermined to decay and rebirth. God has His reasons and they are born of spirit. Your spirit will reveal the reasons in time. Ask in prayer for this understanding and it will be granted. I Raphael, charged with healing, will take your request to the Great I Am for further understanding so that consultation may be given. Remember we are God's emissaries of his mercy and love.

*OK take your hand and **curl it** and make like a tube effect **to look** through. See you only see a **little of the reality** that is **really** around you. Concentrate of that **tiny area** you truly **see.** Now stretched out your hand and put it down at your side. Now look at the huge reality **around** that little bit **that you saw**. Take a few minutes to look around.....Now remember to do this when you don't understand something or someone and remember also that... like your curled hand you only see a little bit.... but always trust there is a whole lot more ....God sees it all so **trust** Him. **Always trust him** and whenever you don't so much.... make that curled hand and look through it and it will remind* *you about how very little you see and it will help you have faith in the knowledge that there is always **more** than you can see and God sees everything so trust.*

Sandy: With My Father's Passing it looks like I will be getting some monies from his estate Not a lot of money but some. I know that I will pay off the debts that I have incurred that are not in my highest good nor the way God wants me to live. The challenge is not to take the blessing of money and compound it to where I am paying Ceasar. I want the money to serve God. I know to live simply enough not to create debt in the first place too. But my question is how to spend the remainder. So I asked God how to handle it.

God took $1000 in his hand. And he held it out and said, "Now in My kingdom what is more valuable, this $1000 or the hundred acts of kindness it could produce?

Sandy: So I guess I have my answer. I will ask in prayer though before I am led to any decisions,.

VALUE VERSUS IMPORTANCE: There have been different things and people in my life that have been important to me in the place that I am and was. These are my importance's.

Everything and everyone has value and thus importance, throughout the scheme of life. Just because it is not important to me just at this stage of my journey does not mean that it does not have value intrinsically. The things that move in and out of my life are important to me right now and have often times became important later. Take my walker. Up to now a walker has not been important to me because I had mobility. Now my mobility is limited by age and so now important when it was not so even 10 years ago. A walker however always had value of its own without my need for it.

When I think of Jesus I think of the value He has given each one of us by His God/Man relationship and I feel deep love and thankfulness. Jesus, as God and human has given each one of us value both divinely and humanly. Just because at this moment in my life I do not hold this person or that person in importance does not mean that they do not have value. It has increasingly become important to me to appreciate the value in everything. I think this is something you see when you get older that maybe we miss when we are younger and trying to put our worlds together. The choices we make throughout our lives give our life importance but God gave us value, each one of us, whether we knew it or not. Value brings importance. When we are younger importance brings value. But when you get older and have lived for some time you see valuable outside of personal importance.

THE "OUR FATHER": So I was discussing with God the second part of life. The part where your body is wearing out and so your whole definition of who you are, or were, is fading. Your body simply cannot engage in life as it had when you were younger. Even in conversation with those younger than you, conversations and purpose changes. The young are busy doing what they must do so I asked God about this second half and it's purpose. The following is what He gave me about the second part. First He told me that the prayer, the Our Father, has within it everything that we need for a purpose filled life. He had me go over it and enlightened me as to how it applied to everything and always would no matter what stage we were in. He pointed out that one of the most important parts, ...give us this day....refers to how life changes everyday no matter where we are in our journey here on Earth. Did He not tell us over and over again to only plan for today without always living in tomorrow. So here I am going to write His words as given to Me.

God: You are always eternal. There is no end nor any beginning. You are, now, tomorrow and today. Your body passes but not your spirit. So, therefore know that your life does not ever cease to be. When your body starts to crumble to make life's transition which it must, it is the time for the spirit to manifest in a different way. Spirit manifest through actions in the first part of earthly life and differently during the second part of life. Both parts are part of the whole, many many times. So this second part you ask Me how to live out. The second part is about supporting Myself and each other through the avenue of prayer. I have instructed you as of late to study and say the Our Father for it is the perfect prayer. Arise in the morning and instead of rushing out to work, etc. stop and say the Our Father to set the day's permission and purpose. Praying in the spirit moves things just as your physical body moves things. You can change things even more through prayer than physically. This is the time when vision is given beyond what physical manifestations give. The second half of life is the appreciation of beauty, purpose of action and the sight of divine interventions. It is like your legs have done the walking but now you know their objective and intention. Prayer in the first half of life is a path but in the second half is the appreciation of arrival.

RANDOM CONVERSATIONS PUT DOWN THROUGH THE YEARS: *God: The way of the Dove embodies gentleness and love. There are many paths to the same God but the path of the Dove is different from the path of aggression. There are those however that are called to that path of standing firm and defending. It is important that you do not see gentleness, compassion and love as the weak road. Love contains power and has incredible strength. Did I not tell you that love conquers all. It has no adversaries and does not seek to control but rather lifts. The way of the Dove does not command that you strike out but rather sit in joyful expectation in gentleness.*

At some sort of prompting (God knows why they come the way and time they come) I decided to look up the qualities of a dove not really understanding why this title. I thought maybe some reference points my help my understandings of these writings. So, I looked up on the internet using "properties of the dove". Well here are the references I found: In the Bible there were references in Isaac and Israel, John the Baptist, the Annunciation, the Last Supper, Jesus's birth, at the temple with Presentation by Mary and Joseph, Noah's Ark, and often referenced by the prophets. There were more but you get the picture. In these references it say's the dove was a presentation of God's Spirit

THE MESSAGE: A LETTER TO MY PEOPLE: *God: There is a time of great famine coming soon. This is a time of rejoicing rather than lamenting because for too long I have watched my people suffer choosing and searching false Gods. I am a jealous God and long for your return. Remember that it is I who is the giver of all gifts both large and small. Do not worry about storing up during this famine, remembering how I fed my children in the desert. It has always been and will always be in sharing that life has been sustained. Did I not share my own Son with you? Look to Me so that your eyes may see and your ears may hear and you shall remember your rightful place in our kingdom. Do not worship Me but rather come follow Me and I shall give you peace and joy. Only when people are hungry do they gather food. I am hungry for the return of My people and they, even though they don't see it, are just as hungry for Me. I am coming to reap the harvest that has always been mine, My people. Rejoice*

(Personal feelings: This is an invitation versus a directive. It has always been an invitation but I feel that what is happening is we are getting too much into money, success, etc. and using them as Gods which will never fill the void we feel and need to be truly happy and peaceful. The famine referred to is a disappearance of those things that keep us **from** truly experiencing God. I cannot tell you in words the emotion that pours forth from the Heart of God when He says that He is longing for us. It was unbelievable and there are no words for it, only tears)

Who is Speaking?

I am both the Master and the Servant

I am the Giver and the Taker.

I am all that you know and all that you do not know

I am "The Great I Am"

I am both the beginning and the end

I am love, light and truth

I am both here and there and walk among you.

I am the "Great Heart"

I both
Conceive and Receive

I am the Master and Forerunner

I am the Sheppard of the Universe and beyond.

Shalom

There are many paths to the same God
and this is the way of the DOVE

A FURTHER IDENTFYING MESSAGE ABOUT GOD:

Let me reintroduce myself. I AM. I am light. There is no darkness to be found. Because I am light you were created. You, however being human do not yet fully live that out. When first man and woman made a choice to walk away in search of more all humanity went with that choice and so therefore you remember only partially who you were created to be. Your soul took with it the light and you are all on the path back to complete illumination from where you had been created. Light will never be eradicated and therefore all darkness will eventually be assimilated into the light and there will be what you call, "a new heaven and a new earth." I make this prophecy because once light was created darkness has no place to hide. That's your journey each and every one of you. That's why I tell you to love your enemies and pray for them so that the light may touch them. That light that touches them can never be removed or disappear. That's the power of prayer, light. Light will bring your journey back to your true self and the journey will continue until all darkness will be consumed.

LOVING YOUR ENEMIES. *God: An enemy is someone of your own making not mine. I have given you a formula...Love your enemies and pray for those who harm you. You in sincerity cannot pray for someone and still have them be your enemy. Remember the teaching on light. Send them light and your light grows also.*

I heard a good little quote the other day but do not know who it said, "That people think forgiveness is a really good concept but usually have trouble with it when there is something to forgive." I laughed because I have been there so many times and it is hard. I found that sending the light helps the other person as well as me because when you are really mad it makes you feel better too.

Just recently I had another conversation and questioning about this word "forgiveness." I had been wronged very seriously I felt, by one of my children and was angry. I have lived long enough to know that when you are angry do not look at the person you are angry with, look instead at yourself from whence the judgment to be angry comes from. So I asked God just what he meant by forgiveness because it had been shown to me many times that turning the other cheek as I was taught just was not a good thing to do over and over and led often to cycles of abuse which only worsened. So, I was angry and felt that I had every reason to be and I tried to forget about it but it just wasn't working. So I asked for an explanation that I could understand. God told me that the answer was this: "**When angry just do not create a counterforce of hatred**." When I thought about Jesus and all He had gone thru I began to see that he never responded with hatred. Not one time. He was never a counterforce of hatred then I read something about unconditional love doesn't mean that you have to unconditionally accept bad behaviors. So forgiveness in part is not responding by creating more hatred, etc. I am not sure I am at the point of total digestion yet but rather still chewing on the journey of forgiveness.

THE STATE OF AFFAIRS OF EARTH: *God: The earth is changing and when the earth changes so does your world and the worlds of all inhabitants of the Earth. Don't forget I created the Earth too. Here are some things I want you to do. Treat the Earth as you would treat your mother. Learn from her and be reverent and respectful. Take what you need but do not take just to have more to put in storage bins. Be mindful that whatever* *you do to Earth you also do to yourself....and your loved ones both here and the future. Just live everyday from sun up to sun set and try not so much to look to the future because you cannot control what you do not know. Just be thankful that's all you have to do and that's to help you be happy.*

Sandy: I heard a Native American quote one day that said, "When you wake up in the morning make a resolve to do as much good as you can because when the sun sets, it has taken a piece of your life with it."

There is also a Cherokee story told that I would like to tell you., It was story told by a grandfather to his grandson. It is about within each one of us there are two wolves fighting. One is evil, angry, lying, merciless, etc. and the other is good, loving, forgiving, compassionate, etc. The grandson asked when the story was over, which one would win and the answer was "the one whom you feed."

UNCONDITIONAL LOVE: *God: Where you are all at on Earth you have and have always had the right to make your own decisions. That is one of the gifts I have freely given because I have given you the right to your own life. That's why you are there on Earth. A wise human both gives and takes advice. I am always ready to give you information but ultimately it is you who must choose. That does not affect my love of you only the love you have for yourself and others. Humanness is a path to divinity or can be. It is a journey to be made. Learn from each other in your pursuit of happiness. Be there for each other as I am always here for you. The trick to living on Earth is to take what I have given* *you and share it with your other humans. All of you are branches of the same tree, the tree of life.*

THE PATH OF BEING HUMAN: God: *A human is the expression of creation on Earth. By coming to Earth you inherited certain body styles. There are many things you inherited: family, a mother and a father, body parts to allow you to live here, a certain story of God and who God is, belief systems, time, distance, needs like food and water, etc. etc. There are other species that have other criteria. You have expressions of creation all over the Earth like the different types of trees, flowers, animals, etc. Each living thing has its own expression in this world. But that is really not important to you right now. You are here and that is where you are living out your reality. All you can be is the best you can be. Humans have been given certain specific developments i.e. cultures, that allow them to function as they were created to do. Always a personal God is experienced through your particular perceptions and realities. God as you call your divinity represents the totality of the parts. That is not to say that there is fragmentation but to say that it is your perception of limited. When you on earth take earth and water and mix them together you create a new substance from whence the water as it was and the earth as it was cannot be restored the way it was because it is a new creation, what you call mud. So, how could you call mud.... water only.... or..... earth only. That is what creation is. Creation is always a composite. And so, there is not only one reality....there is only all.*

LITERRALY BODY LANGUAGE: Let me share an experience here that testifies that each thing has a voice even though it does not have maybe a language. During my career at Children's Hospital I took some Holistic classes since I was in that Department. The class I was taking was a Healing Touch class. One of the exercises was to partner with someone and do what they call scanning the body for areas that need attention. The girl who I was scanning was a stranger to me and when I went to scan her body (she was standing up at the time) I was scanning her left side which included her left arm and when I reached the hand part suddenly I heard, "lost rings, lost rings". It was as though her fingers were talking to me. Well, I completely blew it off as one of those weird things and not wanting to look a fool in class, dismissed it. The class proceeded as normal but when we got to the end and we were leaving I thanked the girl for allowing me to work on her and I told her what happened. She grabbed my arm in disbelief and shared with me that she had lost her wedding rings two days earlier and was so upset because she had not found them yet. The confirmation for me was that everything can communicate in one way or another. I have thought for a long time that everything does communicate, we just don't know the language and that day what I suspected became a reality.

GENEROSITY: God: Everyday there are choices brought before you that can change people's lives. Sometimes you are so busy that you do not even see them. Sometimes you are counting the costs and decide you cannot afford it be it time, energy, money or touch. Be more attentive to those in need and so shall your needs, real needs, be attended to. For within each soul is the scream to make a difference. Those are the ones living in true poverty. Real poverty is not seeing yourself as being needy. This man is happy.

He feels fulfilled. Pay attention to your own need to be needed with the realization that you yourself are needy. Feed the desire within yourself for alleviating your own poverty. There I will be.

SICKNESS: God: *is a physical manifestation of pain or a situation that is not standard within the body. You know however the body and the mind act as one in most all situations in which the body may find itself. Therefore the two are not separate but rather different demonstrations. i.e. stress puts a stress also on the body and vice versa. Additionally everyone is born with an inclination to some sort of body weakness due to their parental baggage. It is a violation to health which is also often linked to happiness. But, it need not be. There is plenty to be learned from the whole issue of ill health. It is both a teacher and an avenue of recovery both physically and mentally. Often the person blames oneself when no blame needs to be administered. You were born into an imperfect world so that perfection can be attained. Because you live in dichotomy sickness can also be a way to health. It has led to much research and understanding of bodily functions as well as the relationship to mental competencies. These understandings gained from ill health have led mankind to a heightened sense of the role of healers throughout the world Healing is often a process. Whereas medical personnel deal with the discomforts of the body, from divinity healing should be looked at as an avenue of perception and sequence of revelations. It play a very large role in the journey of enlightenment and humbleness. Sometimes to be perfect, is to be imperfect or deficient often leading to a different plane of consideration and tolerance. This is seldom welcomed initially but may give way to blessings unseen. Many times perfection is what we strive for and I am telling you that* *often imperfection is a greater teacher. It can teach tolerance, compassion, empathy, acceptance, conversion, transformation, reliance, faith and activate a higher state of self. It can impact the world on a much different level than flawlessness.*

YOUR COUNTRY IS IN TROUBLE: *God: You are part of the trouble it's your country also isn't it? The government is in no more trouble than most of you are in. The problem is that most of you are living in the same problem on a personal level. That is... you live on what you really do not have and are living on credit. That is what is wrong at the personal level and the governmental level. You are falling apart because you live on a promise instead of what is really before you. You are living on credit that is really not real. Eventually there is a payoff period This whole idea that you have what is promised instead of what really is.... leads to over commitment to something you really do not have in the first place. It' the same problem with almost everything. I am talking about your health and your way of life on the larger scale. You destroy the earth and its resources and then you spend a lot of money making yourselves well healthy again when you are killing earth's resources designed for your health and wellbeing. It also sets up some to be rich and some to be poor based on that same promise. Instead of living a life of sharing what you really do have, big corporations want you to live on what seems promised. That is why the rich get richer and the poor get poorer. So here is a formula that is real and a formula that will **not lead** you to destruction of those gifts that are really yours. **Live on what you have and help each other tangibly with that**. If help arrives on an individual level and if you really believed it than there will be no need for big corporations that make you pay more than you* *really can spend and would not make their money off you **who are already in trouble**. The earth was designed to live from sun up to sun down. It was **not** meant for you to live in January with the promise of April. See now a one dollar bill is not really a one dollar bill but rather fifty cents because half of it is going to the promise which is not real and all you keep doing is funding the system that is failing. More is better only when you have the money for more instead of what part of the promised money you qualify for. This over commitment has led to the destruction of the earth, time, energy, family life, health and well-being, etc. Start living in the reality of what you really have instead of what is promised. You all do it and you are part of the problem yourself so start being part of the solution. You yourself are the only one who can change it for you and your loved ones.*

*Another part of the problem you have seen yourself in your own building. Someone could no longer afford to pay for their residence and therefore had to declare bankruptcy. He was able to walk away but left many good things in the apartment that could have helped someone else. Yesterday the bank sent someone to clean out that apartment, throwing good things in the trash that someone else could have used that needed it. There was no recycling process only trash. You have too much trash as a country. You raising your own 13 children has seen the survival rate of your own family in relation to "making due" and wisely using resources versus trash. See in your own life where this can be reversed. **Treasure** what has been given you and when you are done with it, give it to someone else to help in their journey. Keep these words before you. **"Rebuild and recycle."** It will help everyone, including yourself. You now collect Social Security* *because you put money into it to help yourself take care of yourself when you could no longer work and become old. That is right. That is right living. This has also help you feed your soul and feed your belly. You have the blessing of raising 13 children this way and you have everything you need and that has happened because as a family you have shared your resources, one with another. I love you.*

ON MAKING THE WORLD RIGHT: *God: More harm has been done in My name than with any other name*. *To make the world right each person must make the world around them right with first themselves, then in forgiveness and compassion for each other. I AM THE WAY. I only love and love does not contain condemnation or judgment but rather unconditional love and forgiveness. Which one can ask for forgiveness for them self if they cannot extend it to their neighbor. What so many of the leaders need is humility recognizing that real power comes from a gift that was given and a commission not to be taken lightly. You have to be willing to accept humility and the role of servant. This is why the true leader usually comes from below the standards instead of above. A true leader has to believe in equality for all therefore assumes the lowest position not to be above anyone else. A true leader looks out after the needs of all instead of putting themselves above anyone. The true gift of leadership is one of humility. A true leader participates in life at its lowest level somehow to understand what the real issues are for all. The attributes one might demonstrate as a leader are thoughtful consideration and awareness. Look each one at your leaders that you ascribe to and follow if the above criteria is the mark of respect.*

The naked soul is not attached. This original soul is not attached to ideals and passions or duty. It stands alone not attached. Nor is it attached to those who stand around you. Not attached to what you hate or what you love. The naked soul is something not easily experienced. It is the true soul, your true soul. Only when you stand in your own soul can you allow others to stand in their own soul. From this place there will be no judgments. There will be no hatred or even what you call love. There will only be you and the naked truth of who you are already. There will be total acceptance of who you are, what you are, and your true identity, your soul. The things that will be stripped away will seem like they are your soul but they are not, they are only the expressions of your soul which is different than your source. Only when you stand alone in your soul will you ever know that you are not ever alone. You will feel it.

You will notice that before Jesus undertook any significant footstep in his course of action he pulled away from everything and spent the time alone. He spent time away to be with his soul. There were no explanations except to do the will of His Father. There is so much that has crowded each one of your soul's. Often the only realization for you, that you even have a soul is only through your lived out expressions.. The soul is not an expression but so much more. It is a personal and real. You do not see the soul of a flower but only the bloom. They are not the same. This however, has been the gift of nature, a place to consider, a place to seek peace, a place of discovery under your personal watchful eye, a place to observe and unearth, a place to seek explanations. Those who are connected to their soul take time away to see. Feelings come from your soul. Thoughts come from your thinking. To know something is not to feel something. Feelings move you, thoughts only set up parameters often thought to be your soul. Your thoughts come often from your feelings but thoughts always come with separations and distributions. I have sent you two words that sum it up......."PURE PRESENCE"

EVERYTHING in your life is personal..... Hopes, dreams, judgments, understandings, etc. "Judge not lest you be judged," because what you judge....judges you....because it belongs to you.

PUTTING YOURSELF IN GOD'S PRESENCE: God: *I do not need your presence all the time as you might think but anytime you put yourself in My presence in prayer know that I hear you. If I hear you I have an invitation upon which to act. But along with that, who do you think it was that woke you up in the first place. Yes, it is called solidarity. The words in your thesaurus further identifies it as unity, harmony, cohesion, shared aims, commonality. A prayer from the heart is always in solidarity.*

..........................*Random Lessons from the Past*..........................

*God: **The Gift of Balance.** I have created your world as such: Light moves from East to West and West to East. Temperature travels North to South and South to North. Light, temperature, matter and space allow life on earth. Mankind with its destructive, selfish ways are shifting the balance. All nature moans in the wake of the destructive aftermath of greed and irreverence and the balance cannot be held much longer if this destruction continues to happen. The naturally created holds balance throughout the human, animal and plant kingdoms. Without balance there is* destruction the thus no life as you know it. You as co-creator were also given this charge, to hold the balance. Be wise and work together because balance is the key to as I have already said human life as you know it.

Take charge of the earth as a gift. Which one of you throws down a gift and destroys it. No, you take the gift and care for it and treasure it. Yes someday you will outgrow this gift and put it aside and come live within your divinity but meantime your divinity is actively living in and through your humanity. Recognize it for the gift that it is.

ON BELIEVING: God: *For you to believe is for you to <u>know</u>. Remember however, that what you know is never the entire picture for there is always more that you do not know.* **What you call facts are always mere fractions.** *That's why you were given the instructions, "seek and you shall find." How many times in your lives have you had to change your mind because some new fact has been revealed. There is always change and change is always runs in a circle (you have a question, you get an answer which runs again to another question). Even the soil you walk upon changes. Even the sky changes. All realities change, leading to a change in conception, which leads to a change in thought.*

I tell you to "judge not lest you be judged." Judgment locks you into a personal belief system that does not have all the facts as you call them and thus magistrates your present judgment.

I tell you that I the "Great I Am" embodies no "I Am Not." When you approach your life with such information you will begin to see and trust that all things fit together.

You ask how am I to lead my life making no judgments? The answer is that you cannot. You will always have to make judgments to live your life on earth. The recognition however, that your judgment is not the whole truth will greatly increase your abilities to love as I love you.

Use prayer as a catalyst. It is far better to pray for a person's highest good along with the specific need because it brings together heaven and earth. Pray that "My kingdom come, Thy will be done on earth as it is in heaven". All prayers are heard and attended to.

BOUNDARIES AND FAITH: God: *What you call boundaries are no more than security points. They are vistas from which you view the world and information. You change the place you are standing and your view is totally different (i.e. If you were standing on top of a mountain your view would be different than if you were standing in the valley). So it is not so important <u>what</u> you see as to the <u>position</u> from which you view. I Am the Great I Am and am everywhere. It is difficult for you to even be able to understand that because there are still boundaries on the I Am because you measure in part through I Am not's. When I say unlimited to you it is still measured in part by the word limited.*

Your world is limited by the word believe. To reach the Great I Am you must not believe anything. When you meditate to reach higher you must put yourself in a position of nothingness. For as I have already revealed to you in nothingness is everything. You ask how you are to live in nothingness.

ACCEPTANCE: God: *There are two words that will help you make this transition. One is trust and the other surrender. These two energies work hand in hand. I need say no more because I know that you understand. I ask only that you "have faith" which is not the same as "believe". The word "believe" is man's word whereas "have faith" is My word. They are different with different energies. "Believe" locks you in whereas "have faith" is open ended. There is no place in all your scriptures where I have asked you to believe. I ask rather, that you have faith which uses* **acceptance** *which uses trust and surrender.*

CRUCIFICTION VERSUS RESURRECTION: God: *Many times when things are not seemingly going your way you pray and pray for the results that would seem good and just and life-giving. The opposite is true however. Look at your realities on earth. Birth comes hard and with pain but yet produces abundant life. This is the first reality of you on your earth and is a clue to producing life. You have seen this journey many times in your and other's lives. Even Jesus was first crucified before resurrection.*

Often times it may seem that things are falling apart and indeed they are. During trying times, painful times, times of loss, times of deep frustration, etc it may seem that you are abandoned but I tell you that it is never true. You are never abandoned. Even Jesus felt abandoned as so many others have from time to time hanging on their cross. But I tell you that never have you been abandoned. Change is never easy and often times seems forced. Sometimes it is but never with the intention of creating any kind of separation or pain. It is rather used to nurture higher purpose and/or enlightenment. It may at times seem like a cruel gift but it is not for you cannot begin to see the love that is being its accompaniment. Everything is in order for it cannot be any other way. This order is often referred to as resurrection. My loving hand is upon you always. Trust Me in all things for I know nothing but love, care and affection and this being true how could it possibly be that any real harm may come to you.

MORE ON YOUR ENEMIES: God: *I tell you to love your enemies — to pray for them — to do good to those who harm you turning the other cheek. This has little to do with the enemy but rather everything to do with YOU. I tell you God and only God has the right to judge. You may believe you have "just cause" to judge but you really only have your own limited visions of what is just and what is the cause. Example: There is a war raging. You do not know or are not involved on either side. Would therefore either side by your enemy? It's your personal involvement that determines the enemy. An enemy threatens something or some thought you hold dear. That something may even seem like My (God's) way and thus seems to create "just cause." This determination has now led you to the making or the naming of an enemy. If you know Me and know "My" heart then you would understand. My heart holds no place for an enemy. There is only room for forgiveness, love and compassion You are instructed to pray for your enemies so that you may learn to love and forgive yourself. Always pray to the Great Spirit to gain the grace to understand your enemy, thus yourself.*

You as co-creator were also given this charge, to hold the balance. Be wise and work together because balance is the key to as I have already said human life as you know it.

YOUR LIKENESS: God: *I have created you in my likeness. I have given you My Heart. That is why I have given you the command to treat others as you would like to be treated yourself. I have put that desire to be treated well <u>inside you</u> because that's also what I <u>want for you</u>. That is My love and My heart within yours. The purer the heart the greater the service. I have repeatedly told you each how it gives Your Father in Heaven great pleasure to give you all good things.*

Remember that it is I who is the giver of all gifts both large and small. Share what you have with others and your own needs will be taken care of. Some are given much (it feels good to give) and some are given little (it feels good to receive) but is as I have previously stated, "life is sustained in the sharing not in the hoarding." Refer to the parable about the farmer who stored up in grain bins but death came one night and remember the story of the happy town.

MOVING MOUNTAINS: God: *Let your hearts always be grateful. The word "always" is the important word for it embodies trust. Trust is one of the key elements in any relationship. Without trust you do not have Faith. Faith as I have told you, moves mountains. Look at the mountains in your life for mountains often obscure the view on the other side. These are of mountains of which I speak, the ones that limit your vision. Ask that I show you first the mountains in your life and then that I grant you* the vision that you have been absent. Pray and ask and you shall receive as I have promised. Trust in My words and in Faith it shall be accomplished.

PEACE: God: *I speak to Peace on Earth. First let me speak to the root cause of not having peace on earth. Let's talk about My parable of the seeds. Every seed holds within it the gift of life. You are a seed. In this parable I do not talk just about the seed itself but rather where and on which ground it was sowed. Two things are needed for its potential both the sowing and the soil. You as part of Me are also the sower and the soil. That's is why I talk to you about being your brother's keeper. Peace comes to one hungry by feeding him. Peace comes to one cold with giving him a coat. There are keys that bring Peace on Earth as it is in Heaven. They are Gratitude, Generosity, Understanding, Interdependence, Forgiveness, Fasting, Reverence, Righteousness, Trust and the Love of your brother and sister as yourself. You each know how making peace with your neighbor brings peace to you. This is the way to peace on earth as it is in heaven.*

THE PLANK: God: *We call it looking through a cracked lens. You see but vision is always somewhat distorted by the plank in your own eye. You each have distinct personalities with many differences and many similarities but different yet. These differences are like the cracked lenses in each of our eyes. You may see the same thing but distorted images. You can argue and argue between you on which vision is correct but in the end it is only a matter of distortions and you all have them. These make for a good world if you are brave* *enough to first realize that you have limited vision first of all and secondly if you realize that looking at your brother has little to do with him but everything to do with you because you are the seer and he probably don't even know that he is being looked at so therefore not involved in the process. That is why great teachers tell you to first look at the plank in your own eye before you remove the splinter in your brother's. Oh my God you might be getting ready to operate to remove the splinter and be shocked to realize there is no splinter at all just the plank in your own.*

POWER

Let Me speak to you of My power. My power

.....holds your universe together

.....holds the sun and moon in place

.....controls the seasons

.....allows birth

.....hold all things in place

.....heals the sick

.....holds everyone's needs as My own

Who could believe that the wind, which you cannot see or touch except by feeling on your skin, could move mountains and shift continents moving a grain of sand at a time. All power resides in Me. You reside in Me and I in you. I created you. War is not power even in conquering. My power does little to conquer but rather changes the hearts of men. My power can change things where no change seems possible. It loves so completely that there is forgiveness always.

I am "The Great I Am in which there is no I Am Not" I am source. I Am love that builds and rebuilds. I move through your every breath and My love moves from Me to Us given your permission. Feel it, accept it, merge with it. I tell you how to use it. It is a power of the heart. Bring it in to yourself into Us. You often pray but you really have no idea, many of you, what prayer can do. You pray feebly when you rely just on yourself. You have to connect to heart to pray in power and that's where I live. Example, to love your enemies is the real power, not conquering them. Stand at the edge of an ocean, quietly and feel it move. Let it move within you. Faith will be built, the faith I have told you will move mountains, heal the sick, remove barriers and bring back the dead to life, those dead to love, hope and possibilities. This is My power. I AM the Power. I AM the Truth. I AM the Way. Align yourselves. It is a gift. It is what moves. It is what creates, but it is quiet. It can part the sea and split the boulders and there are no limits to its strengths because before it no limits stand.

SIMPLICITY: God: *You have it heard, "Live Simply so others can simply live." This is a both a global call and an individual journey. Each of your lives are different and so that call to simplicity is divergent. Consumerism is not an issue in some* countries, those called 3rd world countries but it is certainly an issue in your country, the United States of America. There is much demand and therefore much supply needed. But let us talk to the basic needs of every human being. Physically there is the need for food, clothing and shelter. Spiritually there is the need for love, trust and relationship.

Food was given to nourish the body. If that is its original purpose does the food that you consume actually nourish or impoverish. For years and years the indigenous peoples survived and lived healthy on those local food stuffs found around them. The seasons were a big part of that. People lived according to these seasons because their food supply sources were relative to that season. Their ceremonies were seasonally motivated also as well as their calendars. There has been movement away from locally grown foods to imported foods which has given a greater variety. The big difference is that in the beginning there was no waste and there was reverence built around food. Today there is much waste and food for pleasure has replaced food for nourishment. I ask that you look in each of your own lives at your relationship with your food.

Clothing: Clothing's original intent was to keep your body insulated against the elements both cold and hot. It was not in abundance with the indigenous peoples because they had to make it, first from skins, then from materials. Much time and effort was put into clothing items and their relationship with clothes was simple but much more practical and limited. Today clothing is often a marker of your status and worth. It was somewhat that also with indigenous peoples but not to the degree it is today. That *is why I tell you if you have two coats give one away. Live closer to your need than your want and it will free you to live more simply.*

Shelter: *Everything on earth needs shelter. Humans, animals and plants also need shelter. Each different but also universal. There were the individual family homes (even among the animals) and then there were the common shelters recognizing the needs for socialized communal living. The animals and plants also know this need and live accordingly. There is a difference however between shelter and living accommodations. Is your home shelter or living accommodations (i.e. that which accommodates the way you are living). Are you in crisis paying for these advances where it has far exceeded shelter? Shelter was never meant to impoverish.*

I tell you the less you need the richer you are. The less you need the less the abuse to Mother Earth. The less you need the more you have to share. The less you need the closer you are to the truth that there really is enough for everyone. It is the distribution that embodies poverty. Be mindful therefore of other's needs in relation to establishing your own needs. Remember I am the giver of all gifts both large and small. It's not the size of the gift that determines your worth but rather the justice on which you rationalize its priority.

SURRENDER: God: *When you get to a point where you have tried everything you know to try...try this "surrender". The sun comes up each day. You do not make it come up or wish for it to come up or try to engineer it to come up, it just comes up. Real surrender is knowing and counting on it and trusting it* automatically. The reason mankind, yourself included, does not embrace surrender is that you often feel that you have to conquer and control. I tell you the only control you have really have, is surrender. Do you not think about what I said when I told you, "do not worry, do I not feed the birds and care for them?" Believe that I care for each of you as well! I am your heavenly Father. You are not all grown up and you still need Me. I have given you life. I care for you each moment...come to Me all you who are weary. Rest in My love and surrender to it. Never think you are unworthy or not cared about or not treasured. Know My hand is on your hearts and minds and souls. Rejoice and be glad for I your Father love you now and forever, Amen. Trust Me when I say the storms in your life are sent for reasons you cannot imagine and out of the love I do have for you. I know it may seem that you yourself bring on these storms often but remember I have also given you that permission calling it free will. That is how much trust I have in you. Also remember that some successes are built on failures that's also why the parable of the prodigal son. That is not to say that you should not try. I am simply saying if all your efforts and/or reform movements have not brought you to resolve, then be honest about it and surrender. Sometimes surrender is your greatest tool to learning so do not be afraid of it as some sort of failure. Surrender can often be the beginning of the success and not the end.

EMOTIONS: God: Emotions were created by Myself. They are tools. They can move mountains or destroy. Without emotions you would really be dead to life. This is how to use them. First, in situations where strong emotions are present, identify the emotion (love, hate, justice, worry, etc). Search the emotional situation's source (why you feel this way). What belief triggered your strong emotion? If the emotion is not something that I would hold in My heart know that it is you that must search out the answer and know that I will help you with that. If the emotion is something I would hold in My heart use thanksgiving and gratitude.

DISPELLING DARKNESS

Let's talk about what you call Darkness. Yes, there are times in all of your lives when you feel this darkness upon you. It can come from insecurities, from hard times, from feeling inadequate or you could be mad at yourself for not being or doing something. So, you work hard at trying to correct the situation. You work hard to overcome. I tell you dispelling darkness first comes with the understanding of what light is. Light does not have to work hard to eradicate. It illuminates. The first thing you should remember is that you are loved, really loved by God Forever. Darkness disappears at the true illumination of who you are. Look in the mirror and no matter what is going on in your life see, feel and truly know I love you just the way you are. It is your true birthright. You will see Me in those eyes in the mirror – that is light. It is a true illumination that comes as light moves the darkness. Accept it, celebrate it and let it give movement to your soul. Hold on to it. Let it sink deeply into your every cell. Things will change and you will truly be able to bring forth the light into yourself and your family, your friends but mostly yourself. Light was the first **thing I created. It is the most important creation aspect I can give you and** continue to give you each day. I am always with you.

Disturbing News, Sunday January 19, 2014

Pope Francis in an audience accompanied by two children, released two doves from the Vatican window on Sunday, January 19, 2014, in honor of peace. As soon as they were released one dove was attacked by a seagull but got away and the other was attacked by a Crow and they do not know what happened to either one. Lord this is scary and does it have any meaning for us as a nation and church? Is there a message here

God: *The release of peace in the world will be met with and on two different fronts. One from across the sea and the other within the confines of the church. From the hands of the Pope and the hands of two innocent children peace symbols was actively set free as a witness calling for peace The harbinger of death (the crow) that is often spotted before battles directly attacked one of the messengers of peace. The crow sits by and waits until the destruction is complete and flies down to pick the dead bones of flesh as does the seagull. There will be much opposition to peace and the carnage laying on the earth soon*

Today

We are standing here!!!
And from **this place** we steer
Our ships of fortune,
Giving us our portion

But the tides bring change,
And landscapes rearrange,
And we no longer know

Just which way to go.

And so we flounder
To rediscover our founder
And know not to whom
We shall sing our tune.

And then it happens
We find different mappings
Places we would not have known
If the "same place" was always home

For life is a trip
To be walked not to just sit
And so we begin to trust
Change is a must

And whatever is built eventually falls
No matter how strong or high the walls
But only to cycle again
Proving nothing ever ends

And so our quest for today
To tomorrow will always give way
But one thing still remains
Time always breaks chains
Here On Earth.

by Sandra Orlando

JOURNEYS: God: *There are two journeys to be made from where you are at right now. The first is the journey of what you will leave with Earth and the second is where we will meet again in Divinity. You understand that something always comes out of something else. Everything on Earth recycles into some other form of being. There is growth and re-growth. A tree produces a seed that produces another and on and on. Even your trash today will become part of something tomorrow. When you look at your earthly experience it would be wise if you would look at what you have left behind for the next generation. It is the way of creation. Make a good difference from your being there.*

*The second journey to be made is your journey back to Us. When you were placed on earth and given life there it was for a reason that was all tied up with your divinity. You asked to come back to become more. Only the angels are **sent** not you children. You asked because you wanted to learn, to contribute, to make a difference. There are ways that you want corrected and/or shared. You knew it would take sacrifice but you were willing. We share such great love between us that you wanted to become more and more Divine. Your earthly lives and your heavenly life are not so separate. It is like an egg. It is all encapsulated within a round shell (life) with two distinct parts. The yolk is your life in heaven, your divinity, your life giving fertilizations whereas the white is directly connected to the yolk but completes the identification of an egg. It is the service around the yolk. The yolk is your Divinity. That is why you were created male and female. The female counter part furnishes the egg (the yolk) and male counterpart furnishes the fertilization (your earthly life). Both are needed to produce.*

Personal Stories of Mine and Others

A Personal Story About Connections - Sandra

Just about 7 days ago I fell on my patio and luckily nothing was broken but bruised. The bruising has not allowed to lay on my side to sleep and so therefore I have gone almost a week without sleeping thru nor comfortably. Laying on my back I have had difficulty breathing at night and wondered if it had not been the swelling or the overuse of my ventolin inhaler. I have memories of my mother who also had asthma being in the hospital and the family standing outside her room when the doctor said that in part she was not healing from her diverticulitis surgery because of all the years she had been on the steroids. I half wondered if that was not in fact my problem because I had been overusing my inhaler as of late. Later that day I went to visit my son-in-law Jeff who had came home from the hospital after major lung surgery. He was very close to death many times but pulled out of it. After leaving his home I decided that while I was out I would stop at Kroger's and buy some vegetables because I was out of vegetables. On the way there I thought about how I had to throw away sometimes the vegetables because it was just me here. I decided that maybe it would be more cost effective to just buy a big salad already prepared and then there would be no waste and it even may be cheaper. I then pulled in Applebees and pulled up to the carry out and placed my order. I was sitting there when I noticed something on the passenger side floor in the front that looked like some sort of notebook that seemed very old because the cover had turned yellow. I picked it up and it was a day to day log written by my mother who had been dead for 20 some years.

Now no one had been in my car for months and it was always kept locked when I was not in it and was usually kept in the garage. Now the only ones that I could have gotten the notebook from where one of my two sisters and I had not seen them in over a month. That book was not there yesterday, nor today, nor any other day either. In fact I had never seen it before. I went home and called Mickey my friend immediately to tell her how this book had just appeared from nowhere. She was as equally amazed and said that maybe my mom was trying to tell me something. For some reason she said that the pages 15 and 23 were in her mind and asked that I read them., Page 15. It was a log from January 1, 1987 thru Jan. 9, 1987. One of the entries talked about her having trouble getting to sleep and having a bad night. The entries on page 23 were regarding her having to go to the doctor and her prednisone being a problem, that was her steroid much like my inhaler. Was it a warning or was maybe it not. Don't know. Just know that this tablet was not there this morning.

Personal Story about Reaching Out
Beyond the Grave - Sandra

One night at the urging of a friend, I attended an single's night in Clifton. During the evening's social I accidentally, or so I thought, bumped into this complete stranger and at his side stood a ghost of a young teenage boy. A first I said nothing, just wondering what I should do if anything. Finally I told the man about this young boy standing at his side next to him. The man asked me to describe him and I did. Then he asked me to ask the boy what he wanted. The boy told me he wanted his father's forgiveness. The man stood there with tears in his eyes and told me that the description matched his 17 year old son that had recently committed suicide. The man asked me what he should do. I told him if it was me I would go to a quiet place and call the son's name to see if he would come. The man left all teary eyed. It was a couple of weeks later when I saw him again and he took me aside and told me this story. He went home that night and sat on the couch and called his son's name. He said all the lights that were on in the house started flickering on and off and then stopped and he felt that his son was in the room. He told his son that he forgave him knowing that he was sick and that he should not worry about him but rather pass over to the other side. All the lights went out then immediately came back on. He said he figured that he had gone on. You could hear the sigh of relief in his voice. He thanked me and I never saw him again, mainly because I did not go back because this single's group was not my cup of tea. I did feel that it was resolved however and that the son did go on.

I have had at least three of these experiences throughout my life so I figure that you could indeed reach across the grave. One experience was with my brother's wife and daughter who were in an accident and one with my own daughter than I miscarried.

Personal Witness to Other Evolutions: Sandra

Another group of experiences are around what we term aliens. One night my husband and I and kids were camped up at Brookville Lake in Indiana. I took a walk along the beach alone just because it was a pretty night. I sat down in the sand and out of nowhere these three saucer like crafts came upon the horizon. Look, they moved so fast and in so many directions there is no way they could have been planes or even helicopters. They would move from horizon to horizon in seconds then zoom straight up, straight down, diagonal and would break away from each other as if they were playing tag. It was amazing the speed. The next day it was in the local paper about these sightings.

I additionally awoke one night with these three beings standing over me. Yes, they were the classic figures you see in the movies. They had large elongated eyes that were black and no clothes and lights at the ends of their fingers. They were working on my legs. I had very bad knees at that point and even later got a knee replacement. I closed my eyes and woke up the next morning thinking that I was dreaming but when I hopped out of bed I stood there with no pain. I went to work that morning thinking that perhaps I had a dream but everyone noticed that I was not walking with a limp. This lasted for several months then my knees started hurting again. I knew that had come back one evening later and I remembered asking them why my knees started hurting again and they told me that the pull of gravity was the reason. I can remember them telling me things but I do not remember talking. So, I have always wondered. I use to joke about when I was a little girl seeing my closet which was across from my bed all lit up with a bright light and my brother and I use to joke about the aliens. So, I guess if I disappear one night and don't come back it's true and they have me. This whole experience is what prompted me to ask God if there were aliens.

There are many things out there that I cannot explain. I have personally witnessed these strange phenomena's and I do think that there are guides and angels to help us with our lives. Most of the things that happened to me I had no prior knowledge of and therefore could not have been making them up. I would not do that anyway. Do you know how scary it is to write all this down? The ego is scared. Sometimes I feel like Noah must have felt building an ark in the middle of a desert. I wrote these things because I was instructed to and really was afraid not to additionally. If these things can happen to me what has happened to you that you are not telling?

Personal Insight on Prayer - Sandra

Here is something I wish to share, an insight written 3 years ago. You know I thought about something in my morning prayers. I asked that God hold my hand and be with me through the day. Then I had this insight. Instead of asking God to hold my hand why don't I ask God if I can hold His hand. It's different. I am not asking Him to reach down, I am asking to reach up. I think it's a better prayer.

The Toaster - Sandra

The other day my great grandaughter Chloe, age 8, came through the door and asked me, "Grandma what happens when you die"? I stopped and thought about how to tell her and asked the angels for assistance. Then it came to me. I asked her to go get the toaster off the counter. I told her to think of herself as this toaster. I related death to the toaster (not working) to the dead body no longer working. Then I told her to plug it in and alas showed her it did work it was just not plugged in. I explained that we all are like toasters. I explained that electricity was the thing that made the toaster work and compared this to our spirit which lives in each one of us and is always there like the electricity. I think she got it because she said, "Oh I get it, just because the toaster is not working doesn't mean the electricity is not working, right? And grandma electricity is everywhere so our spirit must still be around somewhere huh"? "Yep Chloe," I answered and for now let's call that place Heaven huh." It seemed to quench her desire for the answer to what happens when we die. I know the angels gave me this because I could not have thought of an answer so quickly. So, she went out the door to play.

In Summation

In summation I am very glad about the times that God and the Angels and I have had writing this book. It has also been a privilege meeting the angels and I enjoy their company. I have cried, I have laughed and together we have shared my life. I just want you to know how REAL this all is and if it is real for me it is for you too because God loves each one of us individually and unconditionally. He is always about peace, love, illumination and compassion. It is hard to believe that even when we are our own worst enemy and often the enemy of each other, there are no judgments from God only love. I have felt His heart. I can tell you that there are no words for it. I wish there were but there are not. I have put down on these pages my encounters as best I could but there is even so much more. Now God wants to say something. Raphael told me that the title "God" is that part of "The Christ" that we access but there is even so much more. The reason you are here and I am here and they are here is....

God says....
*I came to set you **free**.*
***You** came that you might see*
*Your **true divinity**,*
*Wrapped in **infinity**.*

Remember there **is** a 911 Angel Line
And it's **yours** to use anytime
And it's attached to the Divine